Weather
Predicting
Simplified

International Marine's

Weather Predicting Simplified

How to Read Weather Charts and Satellite Images

Michael William Carr

International Marine / McGraw-Hill

Camden, Maine • New York • San Francisco • Washington, D.C. • Auckland • Bogotá • Caracas • Lisbon • London •
Madrid • Mexico City • Milan • Montreal • New Delhi • San Juan • Singapore • Sydney • Tokyo • Toronto

International Marine

A Division of The McGraw-Hill Companies

10 9 8 7 6 5 4 3 2 1

Library of Congress Cataloging-in-Publication Data
Carr, Michael William
        International Marine's weather predicting simplified :
how to read weather charts and satellite images /
Michael William Carr.
            p.   cm.
        Includes bibliographical references and index.
        ISBN 0-07-012031-5
        1. Marine meteorology. 2. Weather forecasting.
I. Title.
II. Title: Weather predicting simplified.
QC994.C37 1999
551.63—dc21   99-14304
                                            CIP

Questions regarding the content of this book should be
addressed to
International Marine
P.O. Box 220
Camden, ME 04843
www.internationalmarine.com

Questions regarding the ordering of this book should be
addressed to
The McGraw-Hill Companies
Customer Service Department
P.O. Box 547
Blacklick, OH 43004
Retail customers: 1-800-262-4729
Bookstores: 1-800-722-4726

This book is printed on 70-lb Citation.

Printed by R.R. Donnelly, Crawfordsville, IN
Design by Eugenie S. Delaney
Production by Faith Hague
Illustrations by Paul Mirto
Edited by Jonathan Eaton, Jane Crosen, Scott Kirkman,
    and D. A. Oliver

To my Mother and Father,
whom I intensely admire, respect, and love

CONTENTS

ACKNOWLEDGMENTS

There are numerous people and organizations that made this book possible. In particular I profusely thank my wife Stephanie and daughter Colette who gave me energy and desire to see this project from conception through to completion. In addition I give great credit to the following people: Amy Bragdon-Roe; Peter Chance; Lee Chesneau; Billy and Dorothea Chilton; Jon Eaton, International Marine; Dave Feit and staff of highly talented meteorologists at the National Weather Service's Marine Prediction Center; Mark Freeburg of Ocean and Environmental Sensing; Mark Lowenstein; Maritime Institute of Technology and Graduate Studies; Joe Sienkowitz; and Stephen Whitney.

FOREWORD

In late October 1998 two significant marine weather events occurred simultaneously. One, an intense low pressure system called a meteorological "bomb" by professional forecasters, formed in the North Pacific Ocean near the international dateline, while the second, Hurricane "Mitch," hit the western Caribbean. The Pacific storm initially developed off Japan and then rapidly deepened, taking aim at the traditional shipping lanes between the Far East and the Aleutians Islands just west of the Alaska Peninsula. Hurricane Mitch ravaged Central America, killing thousands of people in tragic flooding and mudslides, and sinking the tall sailing ship *Fantome*, which was attempting to dodge the storm at sea.

Before the Pacific "bomb" spent its energy across the Central Pacific and finally weakened into a harmless low pressure area, it severely damaged five commercial vessels and their cargo, resulting in the loss or damage of over 400 containers at an estimated cost of over $100 million. At the same time, Hurricane Mitch claimed all 31 hands on board *Fantome*.

Both outcomes could have been avoided with better attention to the weather. In both cases, the vessels missed the chance to evade the storm and were committed to the elements. The differences between the commercial vessels and the *Fantome* are also instructive. As a rule, commercial mariners receive the necessary weather information, moni-

tor the weather consistently, and are practiced at its interpretation. However, the intense pressure to make port on schedule creates a powerful incentive in the shipping industry not to deviate from a standard shipping lane, even when it falls well inside a storm track. Commercial mariners knowingly and routinely "push the envelope." In this case earlier adjustments or course changes could have spared those five vessels enormous damage. A subtle error in weather judgment had devastating results.

The last maneuvers of the *Fantome* suggest that her crew were not in possession of complete weather information. It appears that the crew did not closely monitor the actual position of the storm, and when the hurricane did not behave as predicted, their options were fatally limited.

Weather Predicting Simplified instructs both the novice and experienced mariner in the fundamentals of marine weather and the tools available for prediction and decision making. In addition to discussing the National Weather Service's marine warnings and forecasts (both weather charts and text products), Michael Carr provides a unique comparison of weather satellite images and weather charts covering the same meteorological events. By becoming familiar with satellite images and their interpretation, and integrating them with warnings and forecasts, the mariner gains access to the most current weather information available for his or her position, thus greatly increasing the margin of safety.

With this book there is no reason for prudent mariners to be surprised by imperfect weather forecasts or local conditions that general forecasts may not cover. Michael Carr, himself a proven mariner, has put together this excellent educational reference for his fellow mariners. I highly encourage you to read this book, become intimately familiar with the marine warnings and forecast tools available, and apply them with prudent seamanship and *safety* foremost in mind.

Fair winds and following seas,
Lee S. Chesneau
Senior Forecaster
Marine Prediction Center
National Oceanic and
Atmospheric Administration

Weather
Predicting
Simplified

INTRODUCTION

Earth's weather is a common aspect of all our lives. Whether we climb mountains, sail oceans, or plan space launches, we are all affected by weather. We depend upon good weather and guard against bad. Weather affects our lives in both benign and dramatic ways, and weather phenomena that directly affect only a few lives initially may soon impact many others in unexpected ways: physically, economically, and emotionally.

This book is intended for everyone interested in the weather, and is meant as a handbook to be used and referenced frequently. Although the book's main focus is on marine weather, it will help anyone interested in understanding, analyzing, and forecasting weather.

Because the best way to understand weather is to visualize it, this book is filled with drawings, charts, and satellite images to assist in this task. Chapter 8, "Integrating Satellite Images with Weather Charts," contains more than one hundred examples of weather systems and events portrayed with charts, text, and satellite images. We hope this approach will help you, the reader, gain true insight into the rhythmic, cyclical, and often predictable nature of our planet's weather.

The book provides both a general overview of weather concepts and close attention to particular weather events and phenomena. Text, charts, and satellite images cover topics such as

- ◆ hurricanes
- ◆ low-pressure systems
- ◆ high-pressure systems
- ◆ rapidly intensifying lows
- ◆ doldrums
- ◆ tradewinds

Although weather events and features may sometimes seem difficult to understand and resolve, they are frequently less complicated than they appear. But a grasp of fundamental concepts—the "big picture" view of atmospheric conditions—is essential.

Our goal is to make weather logical, intuitive, and thus understandable. A weather analysis or forecast makes use of all data at hand. Successful analysis and forecasting, however, depends on proper use of data, both in quantity and quality. This is probably the most difficult aspect of meteorology. According to Edward Tufte, "there are right ways and wrong ways to show data, there are displays that reveal the truth and displays that do not" (*Visual Display of Quantitative Information*). Proper presentation of information is crucial in decision making, and "logic of display must reflect logic of clear and precise thinking" (*Visual Explanations*). These statements precisely articulate the purpose of this book: to help you, the reader, grasp and internalize the concepts and behavior patterns of our planet's weather.

Listening to official weather reports provides

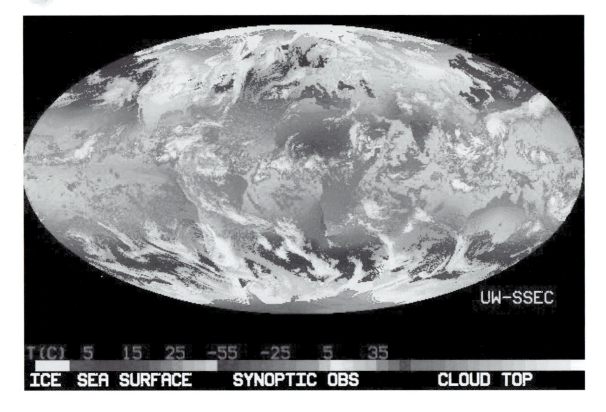

ICE SEA SURFACE   SYNOPTIC OBS   CLOUD TOP

Weather features and events across the Earth's surface and throughout its atmosphere are interconnected parts of a continual global process of heat transfer. We routinely view weather events, such as the passage of high- and low-pressure systems, as isolated phenomena, but they are better understood when first viewed in their global perspective.

you with one interpretation of data, presented in a way designed to satisfy the varying needs and levels of understanding of many users. We hope this book will serve your specific weather needs better by providing a logical and understandable view of meteorological concepts and information so you will be able to analyze, interpret, and forecast the weather on your own. Official forecasts then become another tool, not the sole source, for decision making.

In writing this book I aimed to include enough technical information to support important explanations, while at the same time keeping the discussion straightforward and jargon-free so it will be accessible and enjoyable for nonmeteorologists. Examples, in the form of text, weather charts, and satellite images, cover both the Northern and Southern Hemispheres, making this book globally useful.

Michael William Carr
Peaks Island, Maine

1

What Makes the Weather?

Our Earth's surface consists of land and water, with water being a thermally stable substance, absorbing heat from the sun without substantial short-term changes in temperature, whereas land is thermally unstable, absorbing and re-radiating heat quickly and with appreciable changes in temperature. Weather over water, therefore, tends to be more predictable and stable than over land.

Additionally, equatorial regions receive more solar heat than polar regions, and if there were not a method of transferring heat from the equator to the poles, equatorial regions would become hotter and hotter, and the poles colder. Necessary heat transfer is accomplished through continual movement of air (wind) and water (ocean currents). The atmosphere accounts for about 60 percent of poleward heat transfer, and the oceans, 40 percent.

Air warmed over equatorial regions rises and flows north and south toward the polar regions.

As this air rises, it cools, with some of the cooled air descending back to earth near 30 degrees north and south latitude, forming areas of high pressure. Upon reaching the Earth's surface, the air divides, moving north and south, forming wind patterns known as the prevailing southwesterlies and the northeasterly tradewinds in the Northern Hemisphere and the prevailing northwesterlies and the southeasterly tradewinds in the Southern Hemisphere.

Not all air rising from the equatorial regions descends at 30 north and 30 south. Some continues toward the poles, descending in those regions and forming polar high-pressure areas. This cold, dense air flows equatorward on the surface, deflected to the westward by the Earth's rotation into arctic northeasterlies in the Northern Hemisphere and southeasterlies in the Southern Hemisphere. These arctic and antarctic winds meet the temperate westerlies in an area known as the polar front (near 60 north and 60 south latitude), where midlatitude warm air rises over cold, dense polar air, condensing moisture. Along this polar front, precipitation and inclement weather are the normal condition.

This rising and descending air within the atmosphere forms three rotating cells in both hemispheres, originating at the equator, descending at 30 degrees north/south and at the poles, and rising at 60 degrees north/south. These circulation mechanisms are often referred to as *Hadley cells*, after the scientist who deduced and demonstrated their existence. Areas near 30 north and 30 south latitude, where winds are light, are called the *horse latitudes*, and areas just north and south of the equator, where winds are also light and variable, are called the *Doldrums*. Winds are not strong in these regions because air motion is vertical, and horizontal temperature differences on the surface are slight. Without horizontal temperature gradient there is little pressure gradient, and thus winds are light.

This accurate but simplified explanation of the Earth's atmosphere is modified by changing seasons (brought on by the Earth's distance from the sun and by the tilt of the Earth's axis), by the Earth's rotation, by the distributions of land and water in both hemispheres, and by volcanoes, sunspot activity, and many other variables.

Predicting the Earth's complex atmospheric interactions is therefore a combination of art and science. Weather is both a cause and effect of atmospheric changes over continents, coasts, and oceans and is always shifting and changing. Good analysis and predictions depend upon a sound grasp of meteorological concepts, which this book aims to provide.

Large-scale weather patterns are often sub-

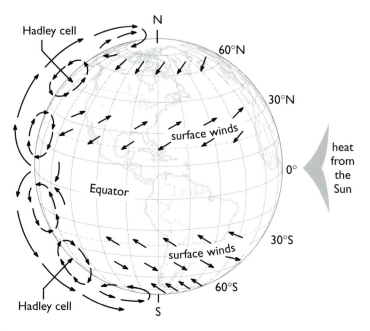

Hadley cells move and redistribute heat and cold within the Earth's atmosphere. In both the Northern and Southern Hemispheres, there are three cells, which expand and contract depending on the amount of heat and cold present.

stantially modified locally by topographic and oceanographic features that are difficult to account for in official, large-area weather predictions. Local variables must be inserted as needed, adjusting or modifying forecasts as appropriate, and it is here that much of the art of weather forecasting operates.

LEVELS OF WEATHER SYSTEM DEVELOPMENT

Weather operates through multiple levels of time and space, awareness of which provides a foundation for viewing and evaluating meteorological events from global to local, or microscale.

We often think of weather as a linear and uniform process, when it truly is a three-dimensional process best understood in its totality. Each time/space scale of weather systems operates independently as well as in conjunction with those listed above and below it in table 1. Several scales of weather can be experienced simultaneously. For example, meso (medium) and micro (small) scale thunderstorms might occur along the leading edge of a mesoscale squall line associated with the approach of a synoptic-scale hurricane. Thunderstorms and squall lines can also be associated with synoptic (large) scale midlatitude storms that have developed in response to upper-level, short-wave troughs (synoptic scale) embedded in long-wave troughs (global scale). Global-scale troughs represent the "big picture" from which smaller-scale weather systems, both upper-level and surface, evolve.

To analyze and forecast weather properly, one must begin by looking at the Earth's atmosphere as a whole. Focusing on just microscale or meso/microscale events will often lead to missing dominant weather patterns. The Earth's atmosphere shows wavelike characteristics because it is a fluid system. When areas of the atmosphere are thermally imbalanced, disturbed by the movement of cold and warm air, "waves" occur. These waves, whose energy is ultimately transferred to Earth's surface, are called either *troughs* or *ridges* and classified according to size and strength. Upper-level waves are characterized by undulations in the upper atmosphere's wind flow with north–south axes, similar to a snake's weaving motion across the ground.

These undulations are a direct result of cold air in northern latitudes moving south and warm air from southern latitudes moving north. Their shapes are determined in each case by the amounts of cold and warm air present and the underlying topography.

Waves of 50 to 120 degrees of longitude in length are called *long* or *Rossby waves*, and are global-scale features. Named after the meteorologist who discovered them, Rossby waves impact large areas and time periods. Long waves influence events such as droughts and extended rainy periods by controlling the formation and movement of weather systems.

Rossby waves are manifested in the concentrated upper airflow known as the *jet stream*, which we discuss in detail shortly. On average, there are three to seven (measured from ridge to ridge or trough to trough) Rossby waves circling the Earth at any given time, in response to the continuous north–south movement of warm and cold air within the Earth's atmosphere.

Rossby waves have their greatest influence in midlatitudes, 30 to 60 degrees north and south, where the most amount of mixing between warm, moist tropical air and cold, dry polar air occurs.

TABLE 1. Scales of weather development

SCALE	EXAMPLE	DURATION
global (Rossby waves, 50°–120° longitude)	jet stream	weeks to months
synoptic (short waves, less than 50° longitude)	air masses; high- and low-pressure systems	days/weeks
midlatitude and tropical	surface troughs and ridges; hurricanes, typhoons, monsoon troughs	week or less
meso (intermediate)	squall lines	several hours/day
small	thunderstorms, hailstorms	a few hours or less
micro	downbursts, waterspouts, tornadoes	less than an hour

Rossby waves have three dimensions, having a varying thickness as well as their characteristic north–south undulating shape. Viewed in cross section, Rossby waves resemble lasagna noodles—flat and wide—with their bottom edges just three to four miles above the Earth's surface.

Rossby waves do not often affect tropical regions, where there is minimal mixing of cold and warm air, but they have a pronounced effect in temperate latitudes, where they assist in creating and steering weather systems.

Embedded within the long Rossby waves are smaller *synoptic-scale waves* (short-wave troughs), which extend over areas the size of the United States and which exist, generally, a few days to about a week. Synoptic-scale waves (50 degrees or less in longitude) control the development and movement of surface high- and low-pressure systems and are responsible for the features seen on surface weather charts.

Midlatitude events, which occur between 30 to 60 degrees in both Northern and Southern Hemispheres, are related to transitions between synoptic features, such as warm and cold front passages. *Tropical-scale events*, on the other hand, occur in latitudes between the equator and 30 degrees north and south, and include hurricanes (also known as typhoons and monsoons, both of which feature strong vertical motion). Tropical events can last days to weeks at a time. Though midlatitude and tropical features are not directly related to each other, they can come into contact as they develop.

Intermediate-scale events are embedded in midlatitude- and tropical-scale events and include such features as squall lines preceding cold fronts and bands of showers within a broad

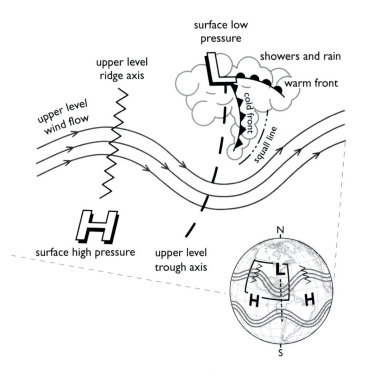

The expansion and contraction of Hadley cells causes an undulating motion of upper-level winds, producing troughs and ridges. Ridges support surface high-pressure systems, and troughs support surface low-pressure systems.

area of rain. Intermediate events, lasting less than a day, are analogous to ripples within larger waves.

Small-scale events last just a few hours or less, such as thunderstorms, hailstorms, or local snowstorms. These events are brought on by strong vertical motion, convection that quickly cools and warms small pockets of air, causing rapid condensation and precipitation.

Microscale events last less than an hour and have extremely high vertical, or convective, speeds. Examples are tornadoes and waterspouts. Microscale events, along with tropical hurricanes, are usually the most violent weather events.

THE JET STREAM

We have noted the profound impact of Rossby waves in creating and steering midlatitude weather. Rossby waves are notably represented by the jet

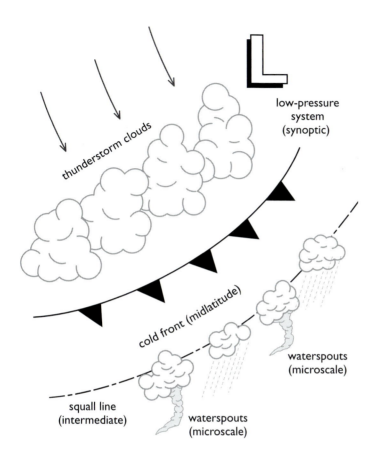

low-pressure system (synoptic)

thunderstorm clouds

cold front (midlatitude)

waterspouts (microscale)

squall line (intermediate)

waterspouts (microscale)

Cold fronts associated with low-pressure systems produce unsettled conditions, with well-developed cold fronts often supporting a mixture of waterspouts, squall lines, and thunderstorms.

Hadley cells, the stronger the winds produced. The full force of these jet stream winds is not felt on the Earth's surface, though, because of surface friction, which greatly reduces wind speed. Jet stream speeds average over 50 knots and often exceed 200 knots aloft; their effect on "jet" aircraft flying between 30,000 and 40,000 feet gives rise to their name.

There are actually three jet streams: subtropical, polar, and arctic. This book focuses mainly on the polar and subtropical jet streams, as they impact areas of greater human activity. The *subtropical jet stream* concentrates around 30 degrees north and south on average, tending farther poleward in the hemispheric summer. The *polar jet stream* concentrates around 60 degrees north and south, moving farther equatorward in the hemispheric winter. Hadley cell boundaries, and therefore jet stream locations, are more stable (both seasonally and through shorter time periods) over water than land, because water is more thermally stable than land. In winter the subtropical jet stream may disappear entirely from the North American continental weather map, while the polar jet dips far south, sometimes steering arctic air all the way to Florida. Come summer, the polar jet may be bottled up north of Hudson Bay while the subtropical jet advances northward over the continent. Through a downward transfer of energy, jet streams steer surface weather systems in temperate regions (30 to 60 degrees north/south).

streams with their north–south undulations, which we've all seen on television weather maps. These fast-moving upper-level winds are concentrated at the boundaries of the Hadley cells, where temperature differences (or gradients) are greatest. Indeed, it is precisely the temperature differences at the intersections of Hadley cells that cause jet stream winds, since horizontal temperature differences produce a pressure gradient, and this results in wind. Wind is the mechanism used by nature to move and redistribute heat and cold, and the greater the temperature difference between adjacent

Jet stream *ridges* indicate a poleward push of warm air. *Troughs* indicate an equatorward push of cold air. Since the jet stream defines a dynamic boundary between warm and cold air, it is hardly surprising that the front below the jet stream is a "weather maker," and the storms that breed there are then steered in an easterly direction by the jet stream overhead. These weather disturbances, in which warm, moist air mixes with cold, dry air, are in a sense the pressure relief valve in the Earth's heat engine.

We can describe the process in idealized terms as follows. When the jet stream has a fairly straight west–east flow, without pronounced ridges and troughs, there is little mixing of polar and tropical air across the jet stream frontal boundary. Without mixing, the temperature contrast across the front increases, and as a result wind speeds increase. The dynamic ridges and troughs of the Rossby waves form and grow more pronounced in north–south amplitude, generating low-pressure systems that mix the air masses and reduce temperature contrast. The jet stream waves then weaken, and the cycle begins again.

Jet stream flow is so important to weather analysis and prediction that each day meteorologists map its flow by analyzing various pressure levels. The 500-mb constant-pressure level, found near 18,000 feet (5,000 meters) above the Earth's surface, is most useful. The core jet stream flow is centered much higher, on the 250- to 300-mb levels, but it extends down to the 500-mb level and sometimes even as far down as the 700- or 850-mb level, depending on the "big picture." There is nothing magical about the 500-mb level; it is merely an agreed-upon level near the base of the jet stream from which many surface forecast features can be derived. Meteorologists have ascertained empirically that the majority of syn-

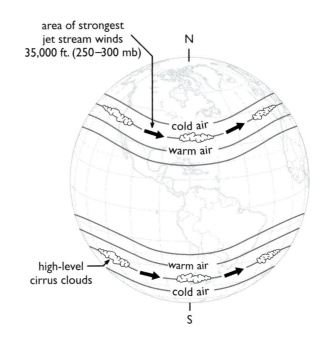

The jet stream can be located by identifying high-level cirrus clouds, which form in the vicinity of the strongest jet stream winds. Cirrus clouds are very cold and appear bright white on IR satellite imagery. On VIS images cirrus clouds may appear bright white if they are sufficiently dense to reflect light but normally appear gray since they are wispy and most light passes through them unreflected.

optic-scale and mesoscale weather events can be explained by 500-mb wind flow and patterns.

Imagine the 500-mb constant-pressure level as a dynamic, transparent blanket in the atmosphere, constantly in motion, distorted by numerous humps and hollows. It humps up where atmospheric pressure is locally higher; it sinks where the pressure is less. Air will flow from the humps toward the hollows, deflected by the spinning of the Earth.

The 500-mb level is depicted in chart form using height contours at 60-meter intervals and wind arrows. These charts are produced and distributed, along with a variety of other charts, via weather facsimile broadcasts and Internet services (see appendix 3).

The location of jet stream winds can also be

deduced from satellite imagery, noting the movement of high-level cirrus clouds (see chapter 7). Strongest jet stream activity is usually found along the poleward edge of well-defined cirrus clouds, which form in response to the mixing of warm and cool air when sufficient moisture is available.

AIR MASSES

Synoptic-scale heating of the Earth brings about global airflow, as just discussed, and also forms pockets of air within this atmospheric flow. These pockets, called *air masses*, are characterized by internally uniform qualities of temperature, pressure, and humidity, and they vary in size from less than a hundred to several thousand miles in diameter. Air masses through the influence of mountain ranges, valleys, bodies of water, and other topographic features, which have both physical and thermal influence on the air that overlies them.

Air masses move across the Earth's surface guided by surface and upper-level winds and modified by changing conditions. For example, a cool air mass moving over a warm underlying surface will warm as it passes over, forming currents of rising air, while an air mass warmer than the underlying surface will cool, sinking toward the surface. Warm air masses hold more moisture than cooler ones, and it is this difference, and the consequent energy exchange between air masses, that contributes to weather conditions. Air masses are the building blocks of weather features, particularly high- and low-pressure systems.

The boundaries between air masses are called *fronts* or *frontal zones*. A front can be warm or cold and signifies a change in the weather, which may be gradual or dramatic, depending on the difference between the advancing air mass and the one it is replacing. Fronts are transition zones, with resulting winds caused by pressure differences. Because air masses differ in temperature, pressure, and dew point (or moisture), the weather always changes across fronts.

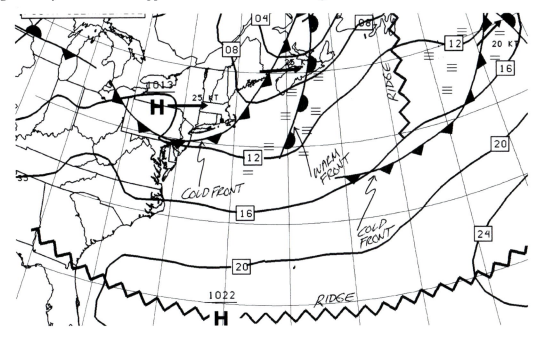

Surface features are identified using standard nomenclature. Shown here are cold and warm fronts, rain showers (three dashed lines), ridges, and isobar lines.

ISOBARS

Isobars (*iso* meaning equal and *bar* indicating pressure), or lines of equal atmospheric pressure, are a standard feature of weather maps. They assist in defining the limits and strengths of low- and high-pressure areas and the directions of wind flow. Wind flow is indicated by the shape and spacing of isobar lines, with winds moving into areas of low pressure and outward from areas of high pressure. If the Earth were not turning and there were no surface friction, winds would flow directly into an area of low pressure, crossing isobars at right angles. The Earth's rotation, however, produces a tendency called the *Coriolis effect*, which deflects the movement of wind (and ocean currents) to the right in the Northern Hemisphere and to the left in the Southern Hemisphere. The counterclockwise, inward-canting flow around Northern-Hemisphere low-pressure systems is the net result of a pressure gradient pulling air into a low, the Coriolis effect deflecting that flow to the right, and surface friction slowing the air movement. Around areas of high pressure the converse condition exists, with air moving outward while simultaneously being turned to the right (Northern Hemisphere), making for a clockwise and outward flow pattern.

Wind speed is directly related to the pressure difference (gradient) within a weather system, as reflected by isobar spacing. Tightly spaced isobars indicate a strong gradient and thus strong winds, while widely separated isobars indicate a weak gradient. A reasonably accurate wind speed can be calculated from a *geostrophic* (Earth-driven) wind scale or diagram, which uses inputs of isobar spacing and latitude in its computations.

TABLE 2. Geostrophic wind distance between isobars over ocean at 4-mb/hpa intervals for various wind speeds and latitudes

WIND SPEED, KNOTS	APPROXIMATE DISTANCE (NAUTICAL MILES) BETWEEN ISOBARS AT 4-MB/HPA INTERVALS			
	30°	40°	50°	60°
10	461	358	301	266
15	307	239	200	177
20	230	179	150	133
25	184	143	120	106
30	154	119	100	89
35	132	102	86	76
40	115	90	75	66
50	92	72	60	53
60	77	60	50	40

At 30 degrees you need 154 nautical miles between 4-mb/hpa isobars to get 30 knots of wind.

LOW-PRESSURE SYSTEMS

Low- and high-pressure systems are chiefly responsible for redistributing heat on the Earth's surface (with ocean currents also playing a large role). High-pressure systems may be composed of warm or cold air masses, depending on the underlying surface temperature and dew point where the air descends and the high-pressure system forms. High-pressure systems are a midlatitude feature, found only north and south of the tropical regions, since air does not normally descend from the upper atmosphere in the tropics.

Low-pressure systems, on the other hand, form at any latitude north or south of the equator and may be tropical or midlatitude in origin. A low can form within a single air mass or from the interac-

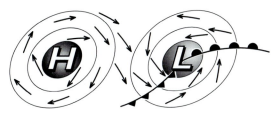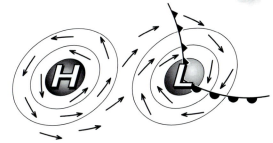

In the Northern Hemisphere winds blow clockwise and outward around areas of high pressure and counterclockwise and inward around areas of low pressure. Low-pressure systems show cold and warm fronts, separating areas of warm and cold air, while highs consist of a single mass of air with no fronts.

In the Southern Hemisphere winds blow counterclockwise around areas of high pressure and clockwise around low pressure, just the opposite of the Northern Hemisphere.

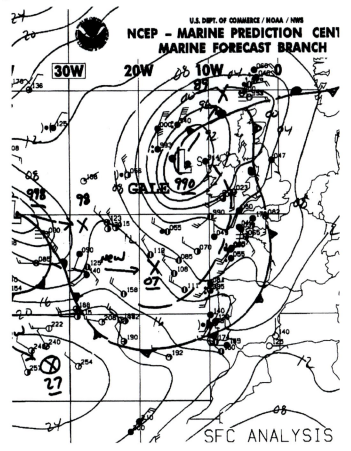

A surface weather chart for 20 July 1998 showing tight isobars surrounding a gale just west of the United Kingdom. Note counterclockwise wind flow, and cold and warm fronts.

tion of two air masses having significant temperature and moisture differences. We will discuss low-pressure systems first, since they involve the movement and transfer of great amounts of energy, producing significant and often dramatic events.

Low-pressure systems in the middle latitudes, 30 to 60 degrees north and south, are referred to in this book as depressions or simply "lows" to distinguish them from tropical lows or tropical cyclones, which are called *hurricanes* in North America, *cyclones* in the Indian Ocean, and *typhoons* in the western Pacific. Whether of tropical or midlatitude origin, lows are a critical cog in the atmosphere's general circulation, an essential link in the interchange of warm and cold air between polar and equatorial regions. As they move across water and land, changing such local conditions as sea state, lows can themselves be modified.

Midlatitude lows in both hemispheres move in a more or less poleward and easterly direction, though variations occur, sometimes including a reversal of direction. In the North Atlantic, North and South Pacific, and Indian Oceans, tropical systems move westward along the equatorial side of a high-pressure area and then poleward up the high's western side. (Tropical depressions do not form in the South Atlantic.) This is all part of the atmospheric mechanism for transporting polar and tropical air masses from their source regions.

The key to understanding low-pressure formation and development is comprehending air masses, fronts, and upper-level (500-mb) troughs. We've seen that an air mass is a pocket of air that is tens to thousands of miles across and characterized by uniform temperature, pressure, and moisture values at a given height. Air masses are often labeled according to the surfaces over which they form; thus we have tropical (T), polar (P), and arctic (A) air masses, which we further characterize as being of maritime (m) or continental (c) origin. Finally, an air mass is warm (w) or cold (k) compared with the underlying surface. In the Northern Hemisphere, for example, arctic air masses originate over Siberia, northern Alaska, northern Canada, and Greenland. The continental polar (cP) air that affects North America forms over Alaska, the Canadian prairie, and east to Labrador. Maritime polar (mP) air in the Northern Hemisphere develops over the North Pacific and the northwestern Atlantic. Once formed, air masses move across the Earth's surface following the flow of surface winds.

When air masses encounter one another, colder, heavier air sinks and warmer, lighter air rises. This meeting along frontal boundaries is where lows form, provided there is sufficient mixing along the boundary to bring about closed, or complete, circulation; circulation is com-

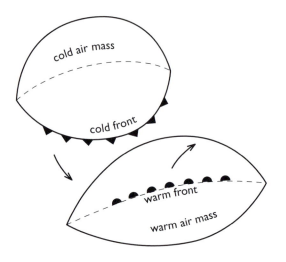

Low-pressure systems form in midlatitudes when two air masses, one cold and one warm, come together and begin mixing. Leading edges of air masses are designated as either warm or cold, corresponding to a particular air mass.

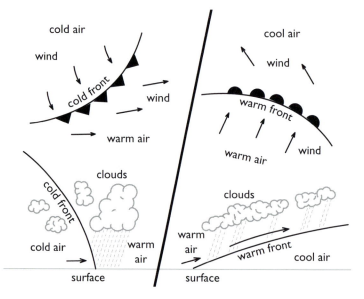

Cold and warm fronts are regions where significant temperature changes occur and clouds and precipitation are found. Cold fronts tend to be more dynamic and move faster than warm fronts.

plete when isobars defining the low wrap completely around in concentric circles. In other words, there must be a sufficient temperature difference between the air masses to promote vigorous mixing with its attendant transfer of heat energy. In the Northern Hemisphere there are persistent lows in the North Pacific and North Atlantic—the Aleutian Low and the Icelandic Low, respectively. Here the relatively warm prevailing southwesterlies meet and are uplifted by polar northerlies at the Hadley cell boundary near 60 degrees north. These semipermanent lows are storm factories, generating depressions that spin off eastward toward North America and Europe.

Low Formation near Upper-Level Troughs

Upper-level troughs harbor the requisite atmospheric instability (in the variations of temperature, pressure, and moisture within their bound-

aries) to promote the formation of surface lows. This instability, the strength of which correlates to the amplitude (north–south extent) of the troughs, generates stronger high-altitude winds, and the strong winds within a high-amplitude trough increase surface mixing, pulling together large quantities of cold and warm air and promoting their exchange across air mass fronts. When this exchange completes a closed circulation, a low is born. Upper-level troughs are always associated with jet stream flow, and it is this mechanism that spawns lows in the frontal zone underlying jet stream troughs.

Once born, these surface lows follow a path and move at speeds influenced by jet stream flow at the 500-mb level. Forward motion for lows is generally one-half to one-third the speed of the 500-mb winds, with a low's path paralleling the 5,640-meter height contour on a 500-mb chart. The "5,640" contour line is thus considered the bench-

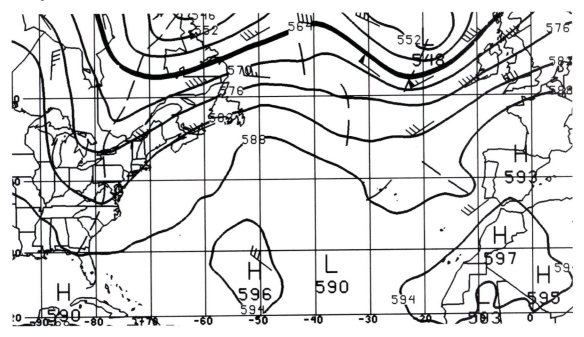

Upper-air 500-mb charts show the location of winds influencing surface weather development and movement. The strongest winds are found near the 5,640-meter height contour, which is drawn darker than other height contours. This 500-mb chart shows two troughs and a mid-Atlantic ridge.

Thermal Troughs

When a landmass is heated it radiates heat back up to the overlying air, which causes air over heated land to rise. As the air rises, additional air is drawn in to fill the void, and this process creates a *thermal trough*. A detailed discussion of thermal troughs is found in chapter 4.

---

mark "storm track," representing the likely path of strong gale- and storm-force midlatitude systems.

Through observation and study, meteorologists have verified that maximum mixing and strongest upper-level winds occur on or just north (within 300 to 600 nautical miles) of the "5,640" contour line. Of particular interest is that Beaufort Force 7 (winter) and Force 6 (summer) con-

ditions rarely occur south of the 5,640 contour, so this line may be used as a planning tool to avoid extreme weather situations. For these reasons the 5,640 contour is designated on 500-mb charts as a bold line.

Surface Troughs and Fronts

Elongated regions of low pressure where air is converging and moving upward in the atmosphere are called *surface troughs*. Troughing is detected by decreased surface pressure, extensive cloud development as thick cumulus or nimbostratus, and precipitation. Surface troughs are found either embedded in tropical or midlatitude low-pressure systems or as isolated features. Warm and cold fronts are examples of surface troughs within a developed low-pressure system, where they are called *frontal troughs*. Nonfrontal surface troughs develop within an air mass, in the unstable air

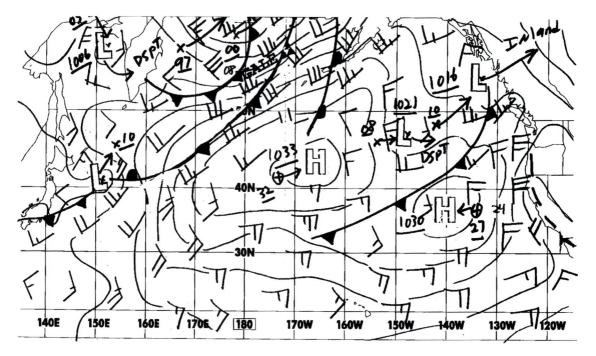

Thermal troughs are areas where local heating causes air to rise, drawing in air from surrounding regions and creating the potential for strong winds. Trough areas are designated on charts using a dashed line. A thermal trough is seen over California on this surface weather chart for 11–13 August 1998.

found near sharp bends in isobar lines and are denoted on weather charts by a dashed line. While an upper-level trough is accurately envisioned as an equatorward dip in jet stream flow, a surface trough is better described as an area of low pressure and thus unsettled weather. There is uplifting, convection, and instability in a surface trough—the elements of bad weather looking aloft for reinforcements. But in the absence of a nearby upper-level trough to feed it, an isolated surface trough is unlikely to develop into a low-pressure system.

Once two air masses begin interacting in the closed circulation of a low, their leading edges are labeled as warm and cold fronts. Where cold air replaces warm air a *cold front* is formed, while warm air replacing cold air is a *warm front*. These fronts move counterclockwise (Northern Hemi-sphere) or clockwise (Southern Hemisphere) around the low's center.

Cold fronts, however, move faster than warm fronts, because they always form beneath the strongest jet stream flow within a trough. Thus the area between the warm and cold fronts—called the *warm sector*—becomes progressively smaller and soon begins to be eclipsed.

Jet stream winds are often strongest at a trough's axis because troughs are similar to the flow of water around a bend in a river. The fastest current in a river bend is nearer the outside of the bend, while the slowest water is on the inside. Imagine a surface low-pressure system as a boat rounding a river bend, with its bow angled toward the inside of the bend. The boat's stern will be pushed forward by the stronger current nearer the bend's center. Assume that the river, like the jet

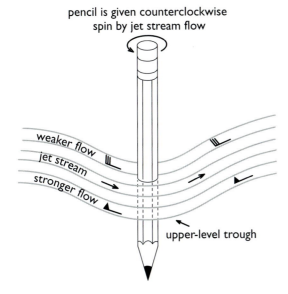
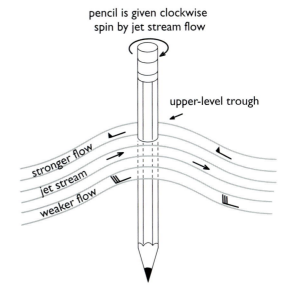

Left: *In the Northern Hemisphere troughs in the upper atmosphere support surface low-pressure development by providing a counterclockwise spin. This counterclockwise spin can be visualized by imagining a pencil inserted vertically in the flow pattern. The strongest winds are located on the outside of the upper-level trough (similar* to water flowing around a river bend), and so the overall flow pattern would twist the pencil counterclockwise.
Right: *In the Southern Hemisphere troughs in the upper atmosphere would twist the pencil clockwise, just as they support the clockwise motion of low-pressure systems on the surface.*

stream in a Northern Hemisphere trough, is bending to the left. Allowed to, the boat would rotate counterclockwise as it rounded the bend.

Another way to understand why lows turn counterclockwise in the Northern Hemisphere and clockwise in the Southern Hemisphere is to envision placing a pencil vertically through the flow of an upper-level trough. Allowed to turn freely, a pencil will rotate counterclockwise due to the stronger flow near the trough's bottom.

The overtaking and subsequent undercutting of a warm front by a cold front begins near the center of a depression, then progresses farther and farther from the center. The consequent lifting of warm air is known as *occluding*.

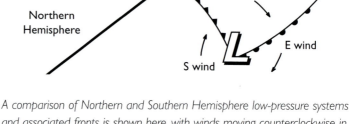

A comparison of Northern and Southern Hemisphere low-pressure systems and associated fronts is shown here, with winds moving counterclockwise in the Northern Hemisphere and clockwise in the Southern Hemisphere.

Warm Fronts

The following features distinguish warm fronts.

- **Clouds** arrive in a characteristic sequence ahead of an approaching warm front. Early harbingers are cirrus (Ci), followed by cirrostratus (Cs), altostratus (As), nimbostratus (Ns), and then stratus (St). (For more on cloud types, see chapter 7.) These clouds will usually break up and even clear out as warm, drier air behind the front moves in, but not before lower clouds (As, Ns, St) bring rain or snow. Precipitation is normally steady, widespread, and heavy, and in winter it starts as snow and gradually changes over to sleet, freezing rain, and finally rain. All precipitation ends with the passage of the warm front.
- **Pressure drops**—sometimes rapidly—as a warm front approaches, then levels off in the warm sector.
- **Temperatures** will rise with the warm front's approach, then level off.

- The **dew point** will also rise, approaching the prevailing temperature as the warm front approaches. The humidity at the time of warm front passage will approach 100 percent. The dew point will remain steady or drop slightly within a warm sector as some drying out occurs.
- The **wind direction** in the Northern Hemisphere shifts from northeast to southeast to southwest as a warm front passes, while in the Southern Hemisphere it moves from southeast to east to northwest. Wind speed does not change appreciably, but the wind is often gusty within a warm sector.

Cold Fronts

The following features distinguish cold fronts.

- The **clouds** are cumulus, and although some may ride 50 to 100 miles ahead of the front, most are found closer to it. Squall lines can occur several hundred miles ahead of a cold front but are not actually part of it. The cloud pattern is not as regular as with the approach of a warm front, and the time of appearance and subsequent passage is much shorter (6 to 12 hours). Behind a cold front there is clearing;

small cumulus clouds abound as the arriving cold air sinks, displacing warm air near the Earth's surface and causing convective (vertical) motion and cloud formation.

◆ **Pressures** will fall dramatically, creating a "V" pattern on a recording barometer. Once a cold front passes, the pressure rises rapidly.

◆ The **temperature** is fairly constant before the front arrives, but falls rapidly behind it, often at rates of 5° to 10°F per hour.

◆ The **dew point** holds steady or rises as the front approaches, then drops with the arrival of clear, cold air.

◆ In the Northern Hemisphere, the **wind** shifts from southeast to southwest before the front, followed by strong and gusty winds from the northwest after frontal passage. In the Southern Hemisphere winds move from northwest to west ahead of and to the south behind the cold front.

◆ **Showers** occur close to the front. Squalls, showers, and thunderstorms associated with squall lines may occur in the warm sector up to several hundred miles ahead of the front. In winter, precipitation may change from rain to snow and snow flurries behind the front. Showers may also occur several hundred miles behind the front due to instability as cold air moves in and lifts warm air, especially over a warmer ocean surface.

Occluded Fronts

Occluded fronts are mixing zones along which cold and warm fronts interact with each other and are either stationary or moving. The following features distinguish them.

◆ The **weather** is gray, dull, and rainy. Rain and snow may persist for days, and temperature,

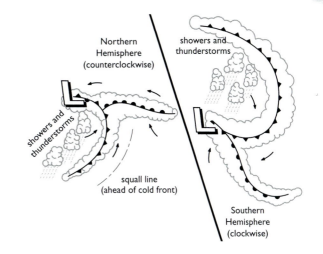

Cloud structure surrounding fully developed low-pressure systems in both the Northern and Southern Hemispheres reveals a distinct comma cloud shape, with a wide cloud band lying over warm-front regions and an elongated tail cloud lying over cold fronts.

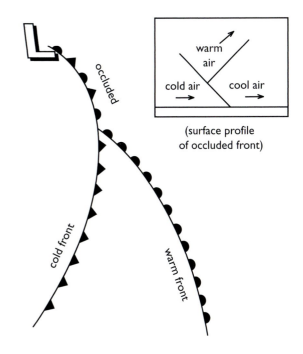

Occluded fronts form when a cold front overrides a warm front, typically producing overcast conditions and precipitation.

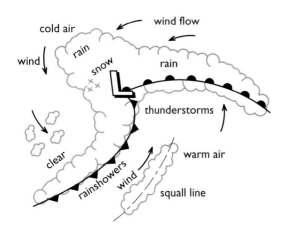

When warm and cold air within a low-pressure system mix, moisture condenses, forming clouds and precipitation. If temperatures are above freezing, rain will occur; if temperatures are below freezing, snow is likely.

dew point, pressure, and cloud changes are slight. Little change will occur until movement within the upper-level flow pattern shifts the air masses. The strongest surface winds are often found near occluded fronts. Clouds are mixed with scattered thunderstorms, and the pressure falls with the approach of an occlusion and rises with its passage, but may level for periods depending on the strength of the low-pressure system. The heaviest thunderstorms occur near the intersection of the cold and warm fronts.

◆ Additionally, east of a low's center near an occluded front rain is likely, whereas west of the center snow is probable during winter months because of the colder temperatures resulting from the north winds (Northern Hemisphere) on the low's west side.

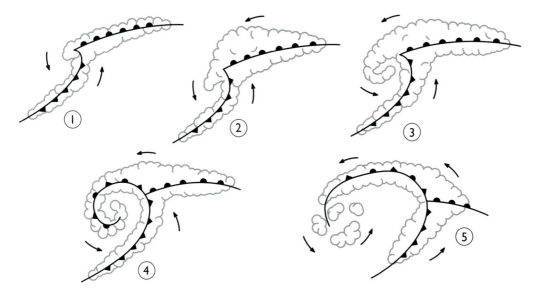

Five-day sequence of low-pressure development. Panels (1) through (5) show daily stages in the development of a Northern Hemisphere midlatitude low-pressure system. As a low develops, its warm and cold fronts wrap themselves counterclockwise around the low's center. Faster-moving cold fronts gradually overrun warm fronts, forming stationary or occluded fronts. Clouds form over these fronts as well as in the low's center. Cloud dissipation near the low's center signals the dissipation of the low itself as warm and cold air become a homogeneous air mass. This basic cloud sequence is recognizable on satellite images and is used to track low-pressure development and movement.

Southern Hemisphere Low-Pressure Systems

Southern Hemisphere midlatitude lows, similar to those of the Northern Hemisphere, normally develop between latitudes 30 and 60 degrees south and move from west to east, following a path prescribed by jet stream flow. Southern Hemisphere lows turn clockwise—the opposite of Northern Hemisphere lows—and feature warm and cold fronts just as Northern Hemisphere lows do. These fronts mark the leading edges of warm and cold air masses and the likely locations of squalls, thunderstorms, and shifting winds.

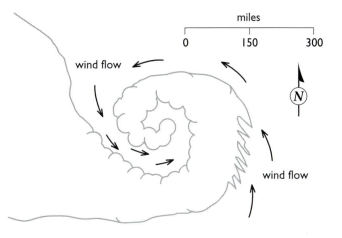

Polar lows form when very cold and dry air moves over warmer water, producing strong convection. Polar lows are normally short lived but often develop to gale and storm force. They are most often detected using satellite imagery.

Because the Southern Hemisphere has much less landmass than the Northern Hemisphere, lows are able to move unimpeded over ocean areas and so have an often greater life span than Northern Hemisphere maritime lows, which are often disrupted as they move over land.

Southern Hemisphere lows therefore tend to be large-scale systems. These *polar lows* are well represented on synoptic charts produced by the South African, Australian, New Zealand, and South American weather services.

Winter Weather: Polar Lows

Satellite observations over the past two decades have confirmed the development of small-scale (mesoscale) low-pressure disturbances over the ocean, primarily during winter months. These lows are small, often less than 100 miles in diameter and rarely greater than 400 miles. They are often associated with severe weather: hail, snow, and winds that frequently reach gale- or storm-force intensity. These lows develop quickly, almost explosively, in as little as three to six hours; as a result wind and seas can build quickly and with little warning. The development of these lows is, therefore, difficult to forecast. Polar lows form over water, generally poleward of 60 degrees, and most often where the sea maintains relatively high surface temperatures close to the edges of cold land or sea ice. Polar lows have been sighted in the following areas: Tasman Sea near New Zealand, Greenland Sea, Norwegian Sea, Barents Sea, Baffin Bay, Japan Sea, Gulf of Alaska, Northern Pacific, and Bering Sea.

Polar lows appear when outbreaks of polar, or arctic, air, originating over continents, move over relatively warm water. An upper-level, short wave trough often triggers the low formation. Upper-air analysis, such as a 500-mb chart, is an ideal tool for detecting polar lows associated with upper-level short wave troughs.

Downbursts

Probably the most extreme type of local squall is a *downburst*: a powerful vertical downdraft that produces damaging winds radiating outward in all directions from the point of impact. Downbursts are not the result of low-pressure systems but rather occur when localized heating produces a highly convective (vertically developed) cloud mass that cools and collapses suddenly. Downbursts normally occur on the leading edges of thunderstorms or squalls, where a great deal of convective motion occurs. Several studies show that convective and downburst activity most often occurs in early morning and late afternoon.

Downbursts are often confused with tornadoes because they produce a sound similar to the roaring associated with tornadoes, and both can occur from the same type of convective cloud. Downbursts can be stationary or traveling, which affects their shape and the distribution of surface winds.

Downbursts are divided into two types, macro and micro, according to their horizontal scale of damaging winds. A *macroburst* is a large downburst with winds extending in excess of 4 km (2.5 miles) from the point of surface impact. Intense macrobursts often cause widespread tornado-like damage. Damaging winds lasting 5 to 30 minutes often reach 134 mph. The macroburst is often seen as a *roll cloud*, a low, horizontal tube-shaped cloud associated with a thunderstorm gust front (or sometimes with a cold front). Roll clouds usually appear to be "rolling" about a horizontal axis. A *microburst* is a small downburst with outward-moving damaging winds extending 4 km (2.5 miles) or less from the point of surface impact. Damaging winds from microbursts have been recorded as high as 168 mph. Macro- and microbursts are further classified as either dry or wet. In a dry burst no moisture is detected at ground level; although there may be moisture aloft in the parent cloud, it evaporates during descent and is not detected upon impact. In a wet burst moisture is present at ground level, such as strong thunderstorms with rain and showers.

Radar is of some assistance in detecting downbursts, as it shows reflected energy from moisture; radar can detect the moisture in wet-type bursts but may give no warning of the dry type. A downburst, whether wet or dry, often produces a roll cloud and heavy mist and spray near the sea's surface as it moves. This activity is often apparent to the eye during the day but is difficult to see at night. Radar will show an approaching roll cloud if it contains sufficient moisture. In general, strong storms with the highest potential to produce downbursts can be identified on radar by intense radar echoes if moisture is present and by features termed "hook" (or "spiral") clouds and "V-notch" clouds. For more on these terms and the use of radar in weather, see appendix 1.

Associated Lows

When two well-developed surface low-pressure systems of similar strength are near each other, a trough may form connecting the two low centers. These systems will then behave in a coordinated fashion, rotating both individually and as a unit. In a related phenomenon, one or more *secondary lows* may form within an elongated surface trough associated with an existing, larger *primary low*. A secondary low (which can be frontal or nonfrontal) will initially follow the flow pattern around the primary low and has a higher central pressure than its parent. As the primary low begins dissipating, the secondary grows in strength and assumes the role of the primary. This entire sequence is triggered by a short wave trough at 500 mb, which is depicted by a dashed line on a 500-mb chart.

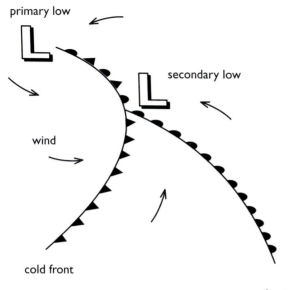

primary low

secondary low

wind

cold front

warm front

Secondary lows often form along occluded fronts, where a cold front overrides a warm front. Where an occluded or stationary front intersects a warm and cold front is called a triple point. Triple points are prime locations for secondary-low development.

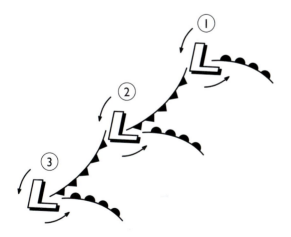

Families of lows routinely form along strong cold fronts, when a significant temperature difference exists across the frontal boundary. Once formed, lows will track along a cold front, with warm and cold air supporting convection.

When a secondary low forms within an established low, an area of reduced pressure gradient and diminished winds develops between the centers of the lows. Clouds and accompanying precipitation concentrate along the surface trough connecting lows. Isobars tend to be tight and the winds strong on the poleward side of the centers or where there is an interaction with high pressure. As the secondary low grows in strength and its isobars become increasingly circular, this wind field and its energy transfer to the low center.

A progression of lows often forms within a trough and is known as a *family of lows.* Typically each new low within a family forms on or near the trailing cold front of the previous low, placing each new depression at a lower latitude. Lows will continue to form while troughing exists, but there must be an associated short wave trough at the 500-mb level to support the process to maturity.

Winds blow counterclockwise (Northern Hemisphere) or clockwise (Southern Hemisphere) around surface troughs and secondary lows and are canted inward 15 to 30 degrees across the isobars.

Forecasting Lows

Two types of weather charts are used for low-pressure analysis and forecasting: upper level (500 mb) and surface (SFC).

Upper-level charts show the speed and direction of jet stream flow and the locations of upper-level troughs, ridges, and storm tracks. *Surface charts* indicate lows (L), highs (H), fronts (cold, warm, stationary, occluded), wind speed and direction, cloud cover (type and precipitation),

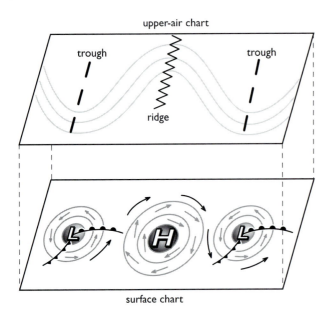

upper-air chart

trough   trough

ridge

surface chart

Surface and upper-air charts are used together to analyze and forecast weather development. Upper-level troughs support surface lows, and ridges support surface highs.

Rapidly intensifying lows are strong low-pressure systems, which often contain hurricane-force winds and have strong upper-level support. This satellite image shows a comma cloud shape associated with the Storm of the Century, a rapidly intensifying low that occurred on 11 March 1993.

and barometric pressure (millibars). When viewed together, these charts provide a dimensional perspective to weather systems showing the relationship between upper-level troughs and ridges on the one hand, and surface highs and lows on the other.

Rapidly Intensifying Lows

A particularly dangerous type of low-pressure system often occurs in the autumn and spring in both hemispheres. Referred to by meteorologists as a *rapidly intensifying low* (RIL), it is often precipitated by a cold, dry air mass moving offshore over warm ocean waters, as can happen along the east coasts of the United States and Japan. When cold, dry air meets warm, moist air, the resultant rapid uplifting forms an area of low pressure. In the presence of an upper-level short wave trough in the jet stream, when winds are blowing at 100 knots or greater at the 500-mb level, the uplifted warm air is dispersed faster than it can flow in on the surface. This causes a rapid drop in surface pressure, a dramatic increase in winds, and steep, confused seas; hence the phrase a "rapidly intensifying low."

If four of these five conditions exist, an RIL should be expected. Using this checklist, RILs have been successfully predicted 72 percent of the time in 24-hour forecasts and 33 percent of the time in 48-hour forecasts. In addition, a low-pressure system is rapidly intensifying if its central sea-level pressure drops at least 24 mb in 24 hours at 60

Detecting Explosive Cyclones or Rapidly Intensifying Lows

Explosive cyclones are the most severe midlatitude low-pressure systems, producing very low central pressures, extreme winds, and flooding comparable to hurricanes. Satellite imagery has shown these storms developing eyes similar to those of hurricanes. Once labeled as "bombs," these systems are now referred to as either "explosive lows" or "rapidly developing/intensifying lows" (RILs). RILs are primarily marine events, occurring in both the Northern and Southern Hemispheres. Most systems occur in the western North Atlantic, the western Pacific, the Gulf of Alaska, and the Southern Ocean near Antarctica.

RIL formation is enhanced by pronounced land/ocean contrasts in surface roughness (friction), moisture, and especially temperature, as when warm ocean currents are near cold landmasses (examples: Gulf Stream, Kuroshio Current). Another factor is a sharp, high-amplitude short wave trough at 500 mb accompanied by an associated jet stream wind of 100 knots or more.

Meteorologists depend upon their computers'
numerical forecast models for short-range RIL awareness. Here is their checklist of conditions that portend an RIL's arrival:

◆ There is a vorticity (spin) value of 17 or greater on a 500-mb (upper-air) chart, with this value appearing between latitudes of 30 and 50 degrees.

◆ This vorticity value holds constant or increases in successive model forecasts.

◆ The vorticity value is located in an area of jet stream flow where movement of surface synoptic features is a sustained 50 knots or greater, or winds at the 500-mb level exceed 100 knots.

◆ There is jet stream maximum (jet streak) of 100 knots or greater at the 500-mb level near (within 250 miles) and preferably to the south of the strongest spin (vorticity).

◆ Surface analysis shows a low (L) with a central pressure of 1000 mb or deeper, deepening at a rate of 1 mb per hour for 24 hours. Please see chapter 5 for details on how RILs are supported by jet stream flow as shown on upper-air charts.

degrees latitude. At other latitudes the pressure drop is multiplied by a correction factor of sin (latitude of a low's center)/sin60. For example, at 40 degrees north the factor would be sin40/sin60, or 9.8/9.9, which equals 0.989. Then 24 × 0.989 = 23.7 mb.

Hurricanes

Hurricanes, also known as *typhoons* in the western Pacific Ocean, are very powerful and dangerous low-pressure tropical systems. A fully developed Category 5 hurricane, the highest classification a hurricane can attain, will have winds in excess of 155 miles an hour and will control over one million cubic miles of atmosphere.

Hurricanes can create waves over 60 feet high

in the open ocean, and low pressure at the center of a hurricane will cause the ocean's surface to rise and produce a coastal surge that can be 20 feet or more above normal.

Many hurricanes originate in the Intertropical Convergence Zone (ITCZ), the tropical Doldrums where hot air rises in the first leg of the Hadley cell. A hurricane begins to develop when an upper-level trough forms a westward-traveling wave in the ITCZ. Frequently this is caused by an imbalance of wind flow, which causes the tropical wave to become detached from the ITCZ. If upper-level (250-mb) winds are favorable *above* the tropical wave (strong enough to exhaust air from the developed storm, but not so strong initially as to shear off vertical development), the

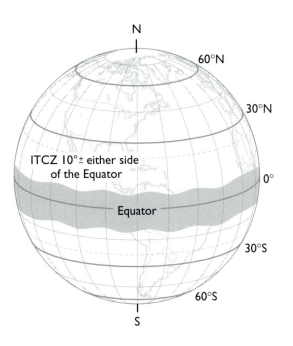

N

60°N

30°N

ITCZ 10°± either side
of the Equator

0°

Equator

30°S

60°S

S

Massive quantities of heat are absorbed by the Earth in the Intertropical Convergence Zone (ITCZ) and then re-radiated, warming the Earth's atmosphere. Heat from the ITCZ is a driving force in the Earth's atmospheric circulation.

requisite conditions are in place. Hurricanes sustain themselves by capturing and condensing warm, moist air, so warm sea surface waters are a further precondition.

Because a hurricane expedites redistribution of heat from equatorial regions to cooler polar areas, it is similar to the circuit breaker in an electrical system. It is so good at removing heat that water temperatures behind a hurricane are reduced by several degrees, primarily due to upwelling of cooler water from below the thermocline.

Hurricanes need several ingredients to form, and if any one is missing, the chance of development are greatly reduced. Basic elements are

◆ A **tropical wave.** As mentioned, this is an atmospheric wave of low pressure that, for the hurricanes affecting North America, has its

origin as a thermal trough moving off the western African coast (see sidebar on page 14). These features are called waves because the isobar lines around them take on the pattern of a wave or inverted V on a 250-mb chart. The waves usually have a north–south orientation and do not always show enclosed rotation. During summer months, tropical waves move into the western Atlantic or eastern Pacific following a path influenced by easterly tradewinds.

◆ **Seawater temperatures** of 79°F or higher. At this temperature the ocean supplies copious amounts of heat and moisture to the atmosphere. As this warm, moist air is drawn into a tropical wave, it rises, cools, and releases heat through condensation. This heat warms surrounding air, which in turn rises. This upward flow of air is reinforced and strengthened by a continuous influx of warm, moist air from the ocean surface, and as the waves grow vertically, they continue to move west at speeds between 10 and 20 knots.

◆ **Surface winds** flowing in the same direction as the tropical wave and at a similar speed. A nonuniform vertical wind structure would disrupt or *shear* the storm. On the other hand, heat dispersal or venting is necessary above a tropical system for intensification.

Hurricane Analysis and Forecasting

Weather satellites track tropical waves using infrared and visible light sensors that locate dense and vertically developing clouds aligned with a trough axis. Forecasters use these satellite data to produce tropical surface analysis (TSA) charts. These charts are also called *streamline charts* because they show the direction of equatorial wind flow.

As discussed earlier, hurricanes develop from the surface vertically into the upper atmosphere, so abrupt changes in wind direction and speed with altitude or time shear (disrupt) the storm's

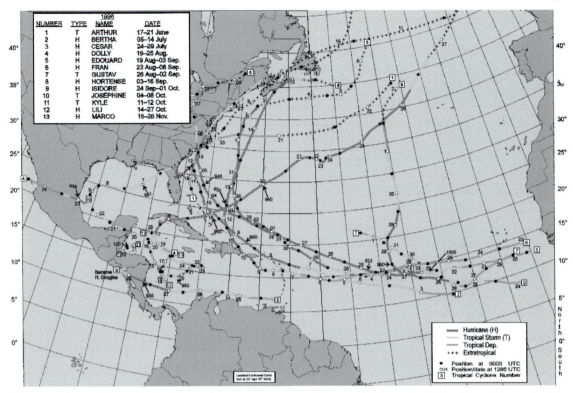

Hurricanes form within tropical regions and move west and then north, following the perimeter of Atlantic high pressure. Variations in hurricane tracks reflect monthly and seasonal changes in the location and strength of Atlantic high pressure.

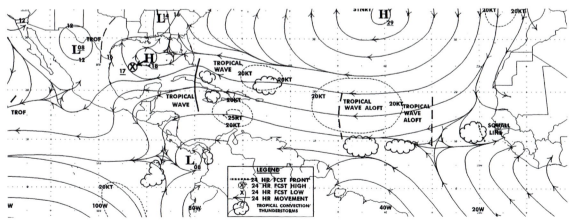

Tropical surface analysis charts show areas of unsettled weather, called tropical waves, and significant convergence, such as thunderstorms. Solid lines are streamlines, showing direction of wind flow. Depressions, storms, and hurricanes form within these tropical wave disturbances.

vertical development. A vertically stable wind speed and direction allows a hurricane to form and grow. Wind above a developing hurricane needs to be sufficiently strong to vent the rising air, as this upper-level flow (250 to 300 mb) is the mechanism for exhausting the remains of the warm, moist air that enters a hurricane at the surface.

Tropical waves usually cross the Atlantic and Pacific Oceans in series, often separated by just 4 to 8 degrees of longitude. The U.S. Weather Service normally issues tropical analysis charts at 1200Z (Zulu, equivalent to Universal Time Coordinated or Greenwich Mean Time) each day for both the Pacific and Atlantic Oceans, showing wind data, along with areas of significant thunderstorms or rain activity. Thunderstorms and rain areas are depicted by enclosed scalloped lines—resembling a hand-drawn cloud—and labeled according to coverage and intensity.

Because seawater temperature is important to hurricane formation, satellite sensors constantly measure it, relaying their readings back to Earth stations. A water temperature of 79°F early in a hurricane season is a good indicator of an active season.

HIGH-PRESSURE SYSTEMS

High-pressure areas exist where air descending from the upper atmosphere meets the Earth's surface and moves outward. High pressure can bring warm or cold temperatures depending on where the air descends, but highs generally bring clear weather because of their low dew point temperatures, which minimize cloud formation. Highs originating over high-latitude landmasses are described as cold, whereas highs forming over oceans tend to be warm. Cold and warm are relative terms, of course, not absolute. Cold highs are generally shallow in vertical extent, whereas warm highs extend to higher altitudes of the atmosphere.

High-pressure systems bring light winds or calms near their centers, where the pressure gradient is weak. Near a high's perimeter, there is, however, a band of dependable winds which lies within a pressure gradient indicated both by tight surface isobars and an upper-level ridge.

There is always a strong gradient near a high's perimeter, because as air moves out from a high's center its motion changes from subsidence (downward and out) to lateral. An easy way to visualize the location of this pressure gradient is to examine a high in cross section (see page 51). Where the sides of a high-pressure mound are steep, the isobars are close together and the winds are consistent and well developed.

Satellite imagery, both infrared and visible, assists in locating high-pressure areas. The centers appear cloud-free and show warm surface temperatures (since air is compressed and heated as it sinks). There are clouds, though, along a high's perimeter, their presence indicating mixing of air and thus movement and wind. Perimeter clouds align themselves with wind flow and are called *cloud streets*. Distinct and well-defined individual clouds within cloud streets are associated with strong surface winds. Surface wind requires vertical as well as horizontal movement, and aligned individual clouds show where both are present.

Strong surface winds are also found beneath well-formed upper-level ridges, which show tightly spaced, parallel 500-mb contour lines, as energy from aloft is transferred down to the surface. Whether associated with highs or lows, surface winds average 30 to 50 percent of 500-mb winds, depending on surface friction and the effects of other, nearby weather systems. For example, a 50-knot upper-level 500-mb wind suggests surface winds of 15 to 25 knots. This concept is well demonstrated on the back side (west quadrant) of midlatitude oceanic lows.

Northeast and southeast tradewinds in the Atlantic and Pacific Oceans come from the semi-permanent highs existing over those waters—the

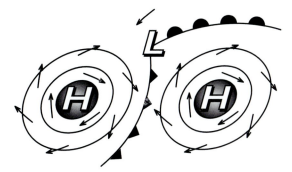

Low-pressure systems often intrude into areas of high pressure, splitting the high into two sections. Once a low-pressure system moves through, the two areas of high pressure will reform into a single system.

Bermuda-Azores High and the Pacific High, respectively. These highs normally exist as a single system—the descending Hadley cell limb for air that rises in the equatorial regions—but they are often modified by cold fronts attached to higher-latitude low-pressure systems. When a strong cold front sweeps into a high it often divides the high into two separate centers, which re-form after the intruding low and cold front have departed. While the high is divided, winds blow clockwise (Northern Hemisphere) or counter-clockwise (Southern Hemisphere) around each system separately.

Ridges are extensions of high-pressure areas along a high-pressure axis. Isobar lines show their greatest curvature around ridges, which are

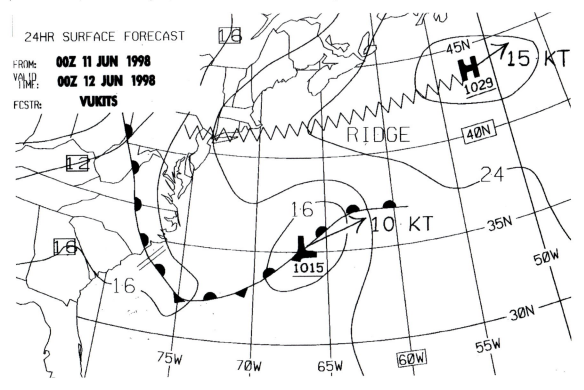

High-pressure ridges are designated with a saw-tooth symbol and represent areas of light winds and cloud-free skies. On this 24-hour surface analysis chart, a ridge lies in east–west orientation just north of 40 degrees north, *and a 1015-mb low-pressure system is found near 35 north/66 west. (Although normal sea level pressure is 1013 mb, this is an area of relative low pressure due to the adjacent high pressure of 1029 mb.)*

mostly cloud-free or have unconnected cumulus and scattered cirrus. Average surface pressure around a ridge is normally above 1013 mb, and often as high as 1040 mb near the center. A ridge, if supported by a strong upper-level ridge at 500 mb, can stay in place for several days or even weeks. For example, when a high is wedged between two strong low-pressure systems (known as an *omega block*; see also chapters 5 and 7), a ridge may last for days.

Ridges, unlike troughs, are not always annotated on weather charts, since they are more easily detected and are nonthreatening. A saw-tooth pattern is the symbol for ridges and is used on weather charts when these features are strong and well developed.

Like high-pressure centers, ridges have light, variable, and often calm winds along their axes. Developed and consistent winds are also found near ridge edges, where the isobars are tightest. Moving too far beyond a ridge's edge, however, carries a sailor into a low-pressure gradient and light winds or calm.

Winds blow clockwise around Northern Hemisphere ridges and counterclockwise in the Southern Hemisphere, canting outward 15 to 30 degrees from the isobars.

CLOUDS WITHIN RIDGES AND TROUGHS

Distinctive cloud shapes form in the vicinity of troughs and ridges, depending on the shape of the features and the extent of vertical and horizontal mixing of warm, moist and cold, dry air. Clouds, therefore, are an excellent indicator of surface ridge and trough development.

High-amplitude 500-mb troughs quickly pull large amounts of dry, cold air equatorward into regions of warm, moist air, where mixing results in low-level clouds and precipitation. Clouds and precipitation occur mostly on the east side of a 500-mb trough axis, where the mixing occurs, while west of the trough—where the air is cold and dry—it is clear. Cirrus clouds tend to form along an upper-level ridge axis, where rising warm, moist air overrides cooler air.

Infrared and visible weather satellite imagery is a good tool for identifying troughs and ridges, since satellite sensors are able to identify clouds by both temperature and density. Once clouds are located and identified, they are correlated with surface and upper air weather analyses and forecasts to provide a complete weather picture.

2

How Weather Reports and Charts Are Prepared

Weather reports heard on radio broadcasts, viewed on weather charts, and received as written text originate from the National Weather Service (NWS) Headquarters located in Washington, D.C., and regional weather service offices throughout the United States, where meteorologists prepare analysis and forecast "products."

These "products" in voice, text, and chart form are delivered around the clock to radio stations operated by the U.S. Coast Guard and National Weather Service, where they are broadcast over VHF and SSB and transmitted as charts via weather facsimile through high-frequency (HF) Coast Guard Broadcast sites located in the continental United States, Hawaii, and Alaska. Weather information is also delivered using satellite communication systems via the International Maritime Satellite System (Inmarsat). Similar products and services are provided by weather services in other countries that are members of the United Nations World Meteorological Association (WMO). The WMO is organized to further weather analysis and forecasting through international cooperation and the Safety of Life at Sea (SOLAS) treaty agreement.

WEATHER ANALYSIS AND FORECAST COMPONENTS

All weather analysis and forecasts begin with the gathering and processing of weather information, which includes

◆ cloud height, amount, and type
◆ visibility
◆ wind speed and direction
◆ air temperature
◆ pressure
◆ sea surface temperature
◆ sea and swell height and direction
◆ ice conditions
◆ precipitation

These data come from ship observations,

weather buoys, satellite imagery, airplane sensors, weather radar, coastal stations, individual reports, and weather balloons. Data are gathered every six hours worldwide, using Universal Time Coordinated (UTC) time as a reference and are called *synoptic times*. Synoptic times are standardized at 0000, 0600, 1200, and 1800 UTC. For our purposes, UTC time is interchangeable with the Zulu (Z) and Greenwich Mean Time (GMT) standards—0600 UTC and 0600Z are the same. For simplicity we will use Z time in most cases.

Observations are coded and sent electronically to collection centers where they are entered into a database. This database runs a variety of computer models, which take initial conditions and project anticipated conditions for a range of times and accuracies. For example, there are forecasts, also called *prognoses*, prepared for 12, 24, 36, 48, 72, 96, 108, 120, 144, and as far out as 360 hours forward from each synoptic time.

WORLD METEOROLOGICAL ORGANIZATION (WMO)

Coordination of data collection is overseen by the World Meteorological Organization (WMO) headquarters in Geneva, Switzerland. More than 170 countries belong to the WMO, and each sends in weather data through weather centers located in Washington, D.C., Melbourne, Australia, and Moscow. Once gathered, data are processed using Cray supercomputers capable of performing over a billion computations per second.

These supercomputers run numerous weather models simultaneously, each model chugging through millions of data points describing atmospheric variables such as pressure, temperature, and wind. Most weather models contain over 100,000 lines of programming code, and even with this formidable processing power forecasts are often issued just minutes before arrival of a new set of six-hour data! Special high-speed data lines, using fiberoptic and microwave technology, are employed to send data to and from each Cray computer so that

within three to four hours of receiving initial data forecasts are prepared and sent to users.

ANALYSIS AND FORECAST PRODUCTS

Analyses give "snapshots" of current weather but provide limited information on future conditions. On the other hand, *forecasts* (prognoses) provide insight into future weather using short-, medium-, and long-range models. Short-term forecasts generally go out to 24 hours, medium-range to 120 hours (five days), and long-range out to 360 hours (15 days) and beyond.

Forecast accuracy decreases with time, so short-term forecasts tend to be the most accurate. Computer weather models are complex mathematical representations of the Earth's atmosphere providing approximate, but not definitive, solutions for future states of the atmosphere; the results produced by computer models must be compared and interpreted by experienced meteorologists.

The National Weather Service currently employs eight regional models, five global models, three ocean wave models, and three re-analysis models. Models use a three-dimensional grid to simulate the atmosphere, with vertical layers numbering from 16 to 50 and horizontal resolution between 5 and 80 kilometers (2.7 to 43.2 miles).

Ensemble forecasting, a technique now being refined by the Marine Prediction Center, a branch of the National Weather Service, combines output from several models to arrive at a forecast. Ensemble forecasting is valuable in predicting precipitation and extreme weather events such as blizzards and rapidly intensifying lows. Global models in future years will have improved resolution and will be run out as far as seven months. The incorporation of ozone and atmospheric contaminants into forecasts is being worked on, as is integration of ocean currents and coastal topography.

Most models are run continuously, with outputs produced as often as hourly. As computer-processing power increases, models are being

Weather Computer Models

There are more than a dozen computer models used for analyzing and predicting weather. Each model factors in atmospheric variables, such as moisture and temperature, to come up with results. Meteorologists compare and contrast model output when making predictions. Often they blend model output in a process called "ensemble forecasting." Ensemble forecasting is intended to use the best features of several models to build an accurate forecast.

There are separate models for hurricanes (QLM), ocean waves (WAM), and climate analysis (CDAS). There are even models that examine other models for the purpose of quality control.

It is important for the user to remember that most models perform synoptic, or large-scale, analysis and prediction. They do not examine, analyze, or predict local microscale activity. A local feature such as a seabreeze, waterspout, or thunderstorm will not show on a synoptic chart. Only local equipment such as a Doppler radar can locate and identify these phenomena.

Models typically have a resolution of 30 to 80 kilometers (16 to 43 nautical miles) and use from 16 to 50 layers within the atmosphere for data input. Some models run within a larger model to improve results. For example, a small-area model, such as the Regional Spectral Model (RSM), is often run within the larger Global Spectral Model (GSM). The GSM uses 28 levels and 40-kilometer (22-mile) resolution.

A model known as the Rapid Update Cycle (RUC) produces 12-hour forecasts eight times each day using 25 layers and 60-kilometer (32-mile) resolution. This model was updated in 1998 to run continually, producing hourly outputs.

Some models, such as the Medium Range Forecast (MRF), are run out to 15 days (360 hours) in a low-resolution mode (2.5-degree grid). MRF outputs have 70- to 100-kilometer (38- to 54-mile) resolution. Meteorologists are currently working on models that will better couple ocean temperature and land topography into forecasts to improve tracking and detection.

---

refined and run more frequently. In recent years, for example, hurricane forecast models have improved in accuracy by 1 percent each year—a significant amount.

FORECAST ACCURACY

Model accuracy depends greatly on accurate initial conditions; errors in the final analysis and forecast products are routinely reduced by as much as 30 percent when initial conditions are accurately reported. Forecasters employ their own experience and knowledge, along with model output, when preparing a final analysis or forecast.

When forecasts do appear to be incorrect, it may be for several reasons:

◆ The forecast is correct and the user's location is

in error. For example, the observer is mistaken about which side of a front he is on.

◆ The forecast is correct in predicting a specific feature but not the feature's rate of movement. For example, a cold front appears several hours ahead of or behind its predicted time of arrival.

◆ The forecast is not correct due to errors in initial reported data. Expect major changes in subsequent forecasts.

In the United States, large-area analysis and forecasts originate at the National Weather Service's National Center for Environmental Prediction (NCEP) located in Washington, D.C., while local forecasts originate from Regional Forecast offices throughout the U.S. Meteorologists analyze and forecast surface and upper-air

Southern Hemisphere "Roaring Forties" and "Screaming Fifties"

Assume wind speed at the equator is zero (there is little temperature difference, thus little pressure change, and little wind). Moving away from the equator towards higher latitudes, temperature differences begin to appear, producing pressure differences due to change in air density, and thus wind. And now, a rule of thumb: For every 1 degree of latitude moved toward the South Pole there is a 1-knot increase in surface wind speed. Thus at 30 south latitude winds average 30 knots, at 40 south winds are 40 knots, 50 south has 50 knots, and so on, giving us the Roaring Forties, Screaming Fifties, and Outrageous Sixties. This rule applies because of the relatively small landmass in the Southern Hemisphere as compared to the Northern Hemisphere, where landmass interruption is more prevalent.

conditions, including wind, waves, fog, and ice formation.

In addition, the Marine Prediction Center (MPC) issues high-seas warnings and forecasts out to five days, monitors incoming data, and consults with other U.S. government agencies such as the Federal Emergency Management Agency (FEMA) and the U.S. Coast Guard (USCG). Information on the MPC can be found on the Internet; appendix 3 contains a current listing of Internet weather addresses.

SEASONAL AND GEOGRAPHIC EFFECTS

The weather in geographic areas with stable patterns—such as the tropics—can be predicted for longer periods than for higher latitudes where weather is more dynamic. Additionally, fall and spring are seasons when midlatitude weather is

most dynamic, since this is when cold and warm air masses have the greatest temperature and moisture differences.

Graphical tropical weather products for the Atlantic, the Pacific, and the Gulf of Mexico are prepared by the National Hurricane Center of the Tropical Prediction Center (TPC) located outside Miami, Florida, and are broadcast via the Coast Guard stations in New Orleans, Louisiana. These products are also found on the Internet, along with a complete listing of National Weather Service analysis and forecast products (see appendix 3). Forecast areas are listed and diagrammed in the U.S. government publication *Selected Worldwide Marine Weather Broadcasts*, which provides charts, text descriptions, and a weather station listing for all ocean basins. Additionally, a listing of all weather facsimile stations is available on the Internet.

Countries other than the United States produce forecasts and analysis products in the same general manner, with modifications based on local needs, geographical location, and weather service capabilities. Many countries offer telephone consultation services and Internet access in addition to traditional methods.

Weather analysis and forecasting is continually improving in speed and accuracy and will continue to improve as computers, models, and communication systems develop. Both forecasts and analysis, though, will always be subject to unexpected dynamics of nature, so users must view products within the context of their geographic area and accumulated experience.

GATHERING ATMOSPHERIC DATA USING RADIOSONDES

Gathering data is critical to producing accurate and timely weather analysis and forecasts, and use of weather balloons, or *radiosondes*, is the most efficient and accurate method for accomplishing this task. Every day at 0000 and 1200Z meteorologists at more than 70 weather service stations across the United States, and hundreds more stations around the world, release instrument-equipped helium balloons into the atmosphere to record weather data.

This twice-daily ritual has been ongoing since 1936 when the U.S. Weather Bureau launched its first radiosonde ("radio" stands for the onboard radio transmitter and "sonde" means messenger in Old English) and still provides the National Weather Service with upper-atmosphere data vital for weather analysis and prediction. In these days of sophisticated satellite imagery and computer weather modeling, the seemingly low-tech weather balloon is still an important component of the weather equation, providing reliable, direct "in-situ" measurements of air temperature, dew point, wind speed and direction, and pressure up to altitudes of 30 km (16 miles).

A complete radiosonde setup consists of a balloon, an instrument package with parachute, and a ground-based radio receiver. An instrument package contains four basic components.

◆ A **thermistor** is a ceramic-covered metal rod that measures air temperature through electrical resistance. It is capable of measuring temperature from -40° to 90°C (-40° to 194°F).

◆ A **hygristor** is a humidity sensor, which uses moisture-sensitive lithium chloride and electrical current to measure atmospheric water content ranging from 15 to 100 percent.

◆ An **aneroid barometer** measures pressure via a partially evacuated metal canister, recording from a high of 1040 mb to a low of 10 mb.

◆ The **radio transmitter,** a small FM transmitter broadcasting on 1680 MHz, sends data back to a receiving station. Experienced meteorologists can infer atmospheric conditions—the amount of moisture or temperature—by just listening to tones from the modulated signal.

As a radiosonde travels upward, directional antennas on the ground track its signal and use elevation and azimuth to determine wind speed and direction. Often radiosondes are equipped with radar reflectors, which permit tracking by radar as well as radio signals and if so equipped are called *rawinsondes*. Another variation of the radiosonde is the *dropsonde*, or *dropwindsonde*, which is used to collect weather data over oceans and inside storms and hurricanes. As the name implies, dropsondes are dropped from aircraft with an attached parachute. Data are radioed back to the aircraft as the dropsonde slowly descends to Earth.

Within a few hours after a radiosonde is launched, its data are encoded and transmitted to NWS field offices throughout the country for transfer to the NWS telecommunications gateway in Washington, D.C. Data are then processed by a Cray supercomputer for analysis, prediction, and preparation of numerous weather charts and products.

WEATHER MODELS

Weather model output is found at various locations on the Internet, most reliably from the National Weather Service site (see appendix 3). Surface pressure, temperature, wind, precipita-

Weather Model Outputs

An excellent display of output from the Rapid Update Cycle (RUC) model is found on the Internet (see web address in appendix 3). Scroll down to "Surface Pressure Facsimile Maps" and choose from a number of 3-, 6-, 9-, and 12-hour forecasts. Information is provided for pressure, surface temperature, surface wind, sea level pressure, precipitation, snow, and 500-mb (including vorticity) and 250-mb charts. Vorticity values, or *spin*, are shown on the 500-mb chart using shades of color. This method of representation is much easier to read than previous methods, which made use of dashed lines. One use of vorticity is to show the intensity of surface low-pressure systems; see the Vorticity Value Chart on page 34 for details.

tion, snow, and 500-mb winds, including vorticity (amount of spin within upper-level troughs and low-pressure systems), are shown in various formats. For example, vorticity values are shown on 500-mb charts using numerical values as well as shades of color.

The display of vorticity values allows the intensity of surface low-pressure systems to be calculated, using the following numerical and color levels.

Vorticity value chart

VORTICITY VALUE	COLOR	LOW DEVELOPMENT
6–12	blue	not noticeable, no precipitation
12–18	green	sufficient for precipitation
18–24	yellow	gale
24–28	red	strong gale to storm
28 and up	purple	severe winter storm

Note: Color value key is often shown along the bottom of 500-mb charts

GRIB

GRIB is an acronym for Gridded Binary Data, a format used by meteorological services to exchange and use weather data. GRIB files are very compact, using an impressive compression technique, thus making their transfer via e-mail and satellite systems efficient and cost-effective.

Weather models produce analyses and forecasts each day incorporating multiple parameters such as surface pressure, wind speed, and wind direction, both on the surface and aloft. The results are saved in GRIB format. Unrefined, these products contain a massive amount of information and can be unwieldy, whereas in using GRIB compression a five-day forecast, covering 30 degrees of latitude by 30 degrees of longitude, contains only 7,500 bytes on average. In addition to meteorological data, GRIB is also used to encode oceanographic information—for example, on the Gulf Stream and other major ocean currents. In general, GRIB can be used to represent any information that has vector qualities, in this case direction and magnitude.

GRIB files differ from text files in that GRIB is eight-bit, whereas text files are seven-bit. This is significant when sending files via e-mail, as some providers cannot support eight-bit binary files. To send binary via a seven-bit system requires using a MIME encoder, which codes and decodes files. There are potential problems when sending GRIB files via satellite text systems using this procedure, as each software program deals with transfer differently. However, sending GRIB files using Inmarsat Standard C has been done routinely with few problems. The Whitbread, Around Alone, and other major ocean races all use GRIB files to transfer daily weather information.

To make GRIB data useful, proper resolution needs to be determined for each user. For example, 2-degree resolution (information for each 2-degree square of ocean) is suitable for long ocean passages. Half-degree resolution is best for coastal application. Accuracy down to 0.1 degree (6 miles) is possible.

Further information on GRIB files is found on the Internet (see appendix 3).

3

Marine Coastal and Offshore Weather Forecasts

VOICE FORECASTS

Voice forecasts provide information on both immediate and long-term weather and environmental conditions. Very-high-frequency (VHF) broadcasts cover forecast conditions for the next 6 to 24 hours. These forecasts are updated every few hours (more frequently if needed) and intentionally restricted to a broadcast time of four to six minutes for effectiveness. Though discussion of long-term weather is normally not included on VHF broadcasts, significant weather features that may later affect a forecast area, such as hurricanes, are often highlighted. NOAA operates 400 VHF transmitters within the United States, each having a range of 40 miles. Seven frequencies, from 162.400 to 162.550 MHz, are used to provide overlapping coverage.

Coast Guard Offshore and High Seas weather products, prepared by the National Weather Service, are broadcast several times each day over single-sideband (SSB) radio frequencies and include more detailed and extensive information than found on VHF forecasts. Since broadcasts via SSB travel greater distances than VHF, their discussion includes larger geographic areas and more detailed information. Additionally, storm warnings are broadcast at eight minutes past each hour on time signal stations WWV and CHU, and on AT&T High Seas channels.

LONG-TERM FORECASTS

Long-term forecasts cover from 24 hours to ten days and occasionally beyond. Long-range forecasts decrease in accuracy with time due to limitations of the various numerical computer models used by the NWS to generate these products. Weather models use multiple variables, nonlinear equations, and large amounts of data to produce a forecast. The farther out a model extrapolates from an initial time, the larger any uncertainty becomes, thus decreasing forecast accuracy.

Long-range forecasts going past 48 hours offer a "feel" or general trend of weather patterns but should not be used for detailed planning. Of particular use in long-range analysis and planning are upper-air 500-mb charts (see chapter 5). A 500-mb chart, which is produced as a companion to each surface chart, shows troughs and ridges within jet stream flow. These troughs and ridges are direct indicators of surface high and low development and should be used in conjunction with voice and text forecasts.

NAVTEX

Navtex broadcasts provide text versions of voice broadcasts and are capable of being received 200 to 400 miles from broadcast stations. Navtex broadcasts are made on just one frequency, 518 kHz, and display or print received weather information. Detailed information on Navtex broadcast areas and stations are available from the U.S. Coast Guard and communication companies.

The remainder of this chapter offers examples of text and voice weather analysis and forecasts, including the many terms and features also used on satellite images and charts. The forecasts are as follows: coastal marine forecast; offshore marine forecast; offshore waters forecast; high seas forecast (two examples); tropical weather discussion; and tropical weather outlook. The examples use transcripts of actual forecasts. Text forecasts in conjunction with imagery and charts allow precise location and analysis of weather features. The forecasts are in their original broadcast form, not having been corrected for grammar or sentence structure, so they can be viewed as they would be received. (However, some punctuation has been added for readability, and the text style has been changed from upper case to upper and lower

case.) Editorial explanations of broadcast terms appear in bracketed italics.

COASTAL MARINE FORECAST

Coastal marine forecasts refer to local time, not GMT or Z as is often done in high seas forecasts, and generally cover waters out to 25 nautical miles. Specific mention is made of ridges (high pressure), low pressure, and gales (winds of 34 to 47 knots). Forecasts are divided into specific areas indexed by coastal regions. To use this forecast effectively, a chart or map showing these geographic reference points is necessary.

Example

Coastal Marine Forecast: National Weather Service New York NY 330 AM EST Tue Dec 2 1997 Watch Hill Rhode Island to Montauk Point to Sandy Hook New Jersey and 20 nm offshore including Long Island Sound. *[Time and geographical area covered. This forecast is valid at 3:30 A.M.]* Synopsis: A strong area of low pressure located over Nova Scotia will track slowly northeast today, reaching Newfoundland late tonight. A weak ridge of high pressure will build over the coastal waters on Wednesday *[A synopsis provides an overview of conditions, essentially the "big picture."]* Watch Hill Rhode Island to Sandy Hook New Jersey Long Island Sound 330 AM EST Tue Dec 2 1997.

Gale warning: Today: Wind NW 30 to 35 kt. Seas 6 to 8 ft on the ocean and 3 to 5 ft on Long Island Sound. Tonight: Wind NW 25 to 30 kt. Seas 4 to 6 ft on the ocean and 3 to 4 ft on Long Island Sound. Wed: Wind NW 20 kt early, becoming W 15 kt by the afternoon. Seas 3 to 5 ft on the ocean and 2 to 3 ft on Long Island Sound. *[Gale warnings are given when sustained wind speeds will be 34 knots or greater. Note how the wind direction moves from northwest to west as the gale moves east.]*

New York Harbor 330 AM EST Tue Dec 2 1997. Gale warning: Today: Wind NW 30 to 35 kt. Waves 2 to 4 ft. Tonight: Wind NW 25 to 30 kt. Waves 2 to 3 ft.

Wed: Wind NW 20 kt early, becoming W 15 kt by the afternoon. Waves 1 to 2 ft.

Outlook for the waters off Long Island including New York Harbor 330 AM EST Tue Dec 2 1997. Wed night through Sat: Winds 20 kt or less. *[Notice how wave height is reduced in New York Harbor as compared with Long Island Sound, given the same wind speed. This is due to reduced fetch within the harbor.]*

OFFSHORE MARINE FORECAST

Offshore marine forecasts cover waters from 25 nautical miles offshore to 1,000 fathoms (6,000 feet), which is, in effect, the edge of the continental shelf. Weather regions are noted using reference to offshore canyons along the edge of the continental shelf. These canyons, as expected, are noted on marine charts. No reference is made to continental landmarks, as is done in the coastal forecasts. Note the wind legend at the end of each forecast, which defines light, moderate, gale, and storm wind speeds.

Example

Offshore Marine Forecast: National Weather Service Washington DC Marine Prediction Center/Marine Forecast Branch 230 AM EST Tue Dec 02 1997. New England continental shelf and slope waters from 25 nm offshore to the Hague Line, except to 1000 fathoms S of New England. *[The Hague Line is the international boundary in the waters between Canada and United States and is shown on area charts running north to south just west of Nova Scotia. The 1,000-fathom (6,000-foot) line marks the edge of the continental shelf, a significant location because this is where the western edge of the Gulf Stream is normally found. Warm Gulf Stream waters modify the synoptic weather pattern, so it is always good to know the Stream's location.]* Synopsis: A storm center moves slowly NE from eastern Nova Scotia today and tonight as it intensifies. High-pressure well S of waters on Wed.

Gulf of Maine to the Hague Line. Storm warning: Today: NW winds 30 to 40 kt early increasing to 40 to 50 kt by noon. Seas building 13 to 17 ft. Scattered snow showers. *[Precipitation begins as warm, moist air being drawn into the storm system is cooled to its dew point. If sur-*

face temperatures are sufficiently cool, expect freezing rain or snow.] Tonight: NW winds 40 to 50 kt early diminishing to 30 to 40 kt late. Seas 13 to 17 ft. Scattered snow showers. Wed: NW winds 30 to 40 kt diminishing to 25 kt during the afternoon. Seas subsiding to 9 to 13 ft late. Georges Bank, from the Northeast Channel to the Great South Channel including the waters east of Cape Cod, to the Hague Line. Storm warning: Today: NW winds 30 to 40 kt early increasing to 40 to 50 kt by noon. Seas building 16 to 21 ft. Scattered snow showers. Tonight: NW winds 40 to 50 kt early diminishing to 35 to 40 kt late. Seas 16 to 21 ft. Scattered snow showers. Wed: NW winds 35 to 40 kt diminishing to 25 to 30 kt during the afternoon. Seas subsiding to 12 to 16 ft. South of New England, from the Great South Channel to Hudson Canyon including the waters south of Martha's Vineyard and Nantucket Island, out to 1,000 fathoms. *[Use a chart showing the location of offshore canyons and the continental shelf in conjunction with weather forecasts, since the forecast regions are designated using these features as reference marks. Other sea floor features used along the East Coast for designating forecast areas include Baltimore Canyon, Hatteras Canyon, and Blake Ridge.]* Gale warning: Today: NW winds 30 to 40 kt. Seas building 12 to 16 ft. Tonight: NW winds 30 to 40 kt early diminishing to 25 to 30 kt late. Seas 12 to 16 ft. Wed: NW winds 25 kt early becoming W 15 kt during the afternoon. Seas subsiding 6 to 10 ft. Marine extended outlook, Wed night through Sat: Storm center continues its NE drift, moderate winds are expected Wed night. A new gale center will track ESE of Cape Cod Thu but only moderate winds expected Thu into Sat. *[Notice how conditions improve quickly as a low moves east. The wind shift from northwest to west confirms the low's movement.]* Winds legend: Light: 20 kt or less. Moderate: 21 to 33 kt. Gale: 34 to 47 kt. Storm: 48 kt or more.

OFFSHORE WATERS FORECAST

The offshore waters forecast differs from the offshore marine forecast in that its coverage area is from the 1,000-fathom line, or continental shelf, seaward. In our U.S. East Coast example, note the reference to the Gulf Stream and the large seas that build when the wind blows against the Stream's flow. The forecast will note any lows forming along frontal boundaries, with latitude and longitude lines used to locate changing conditions.

First indications of changing or developing low- or high-pressure systems in a forecast area will be cloud activity along fronts, changes in barometric pressure, changes in wind speed and direction, and wave activity.

Example

Offshore Waters Forecast: National Weather Service Washington DC Marine Prediction Center/Marine Forecast Branch 315 AM EST Tue Dec 02 1997. W Central N Atlc continental shelf and slope waters beyond 20 nm offshore S and E of 1,000 FMS to 65W. *[This forecast is produced by the Marine Prediction Center and covers the western and central Atlantic waters, from the 1,000-fathom contour of the continental slope—the edge of the continental shelf—out to 65 west longitude.]*

Synopsis: A storm center intensifies across the Western Canadian Maritimes *[Nova Scotia, Newfoundland, and Labrador]* today and tonight as it continues moving slowly NE. High pres slowly builds across the W part tonight and Wed.

Hudson Canyon to Baltimore Canyon *[area south of Long Island to Delaware Bay].* Gale warning, today NW winds 25 to 35 kt. Seas building 10 to 14 ft. tonight in NW winds 25 to 35 kt early diminishing to 20 to 25 kt late. Seas subsiding 7 to 11 ft late. Wed NW winds 20 to 25 early becoming W 10 to 15 during the afternoon. Seas subsiding 4 to 7 ft late. *[Conditions improve as the low moves east and the wind shifts to west. The decrease in wind speed as well as a reduction in fetch bring about a drop in wave height.]* Baltimore Canyon to Hatteras Canyon *[the area from the Chesapeake Bay entrance to south of Cape Hatteras].* Today, NW winds 25 to 30 kt. Seas 6 to 10 ft. Tonight NW winds 25 to 30 kt early diminishing to 15 kt late. Seas subsiding 4 to 6 ft late. Wed NW winds 15 kt early becoming SW 10 to 15 kt during the afternoon. Seas 3 to 5 ft. Hatteras Canyon to Blake Ridge *[the area south of Cape Hatteras to the*

South Carolina–Georgia border]. Today N winds 15 to 20 kt. Seas 5 to 9 ft. Tonight N winds 15 to 20 kt early diminishing to variable 10 kt late. Seas subsiding to 2 to 4 ft late. Wed, variable winds 10 kt early becoming SW 15 to 20 kt during the afternoon. Seas 3 to 5 ft. S and E of 1,000 FMS *[south and east of 1,000 fathoms, the edge of the continental shelf].* Storm warning N of 38N E of 70W and in N wall of Gulf Stream *[the north wall is the north edge of the Gulf Stream, where the warm Stream waters modify local weather patterns]* 38N 70W to 39N 65W, gale warning elsewhere. E of 74W N of 38N E of 70W today NW winds increasing to 40 to 50 kt by afternoon except up to 60 kt N wall of Gulf Stream. Seas building 18 to 24 ft except up to 32 ft N wall of Gulf Stream. *[There will be higher winds and seas in the Gulf Stream when the wind blows against the current flow and warm air over the stream enhances convective activity.]* Scattered showers and squalls. *[Squalls are often intense along the Gulf Stream's edge where large, sharp air and water temperature changes occur.]* Tonight NW winds diminishing to 30 to 40 kt except up to 50 kt N wall of Gulf Stream. Seas 18 to 24 ft except up to 32 ft N wall of Gulf Stream during the evening. Showers diminishing late. Wed NW winds diminishing to 20 to 30 kt during the afternoon. Seas subsiding 12 to 16 ft late. S of 38N, today NW winds 30 to 40 kt except 20 to 30 kt W of 74W. Seas 12 to 21 ft. Scattered showers and a few squalls NE part. *["NE part" refers to the northeast portion of the forecast area. It is important to know the geographical boundaries for each forecast.]* Tonight NW winds diminishing to 20 to 30 kt late except 10 to 15 kt W of 74W. Seas 12 to 21 ft subsiding 7 to 12 ft W of 74W late. *[Latitude and longitude designate boundaries for changing wind and sea conditions, as these are the only reference marks at sea.]* Wed winds becoming W 15 to 20 kt except 10 to 20 kt W of 74W. Seas subsiding 8 to 15 ft except 5 to 8 ft W of 74W. *[The given sea heights are "significant height," which is the average height of the highest third of the waves. For every 100 waves measured in a given area, the average height of the highest 33 yields the significant wave height.]* Marine extended outlook Wed night through Sat night: High pressure moves rapidly SE of the waters *[forecast waters under consideration]* Wed night and Thu. Another front approaches from the W with light to moderate winds. Fri and Sat low pres develops on the front *[new low-pressure systems, often called "secondary lows," may form along frontal boundaries, where a significant difference in air temperature and moisture exists]* across SW waters then moves NE on Fri with moderate to gale force winds expected. Wind legend: Light: 10 kt or less. Moderate: 21 to 33 kt. Gale: 34 to 47 kt. Storm: 48 kt or more.

HIGH SEAS FORECAST (HSF)

These text forecasts look out 36 hours and are prepared every six hours for both the North Pacific and North Atlantic. Initial conditions are based on surface analysis, satellite interpretation, and SSMI (Special Sensor Microwave Imagery); such conditions include winds and seas associated with significant extratropical lows and tropical cyclones across the warning area.

The first part of the high seas forecast (HSF) describes "warnings" in effect for systems with sustained winds of 34 knots or greater. The term "gale" refers to extratropical (mid-latitude) lows with 1-minute-maximum sustained winds ranging from 34 knots (39 mph) to 47 knots (54 mph). A "storm" refers to an extratropical low with sustained winds of 48 knots (55 mph) or greater. The emphasis is on expected trends, movement, and 36-hour forecasts of position and conditions. The high seas forecast contains less detail than the offshore waters forecast.

The second part of the HSF consists of the "Synopsis and Forecast" section, which describes weather systems that don't meet the warning criteria. Systems producing winds of at least 25 knots and seas of 8 feet will be highlighted, including their initial and 36-hour forecast positions along with associated conditions if appropriate. In addition, the "Synopsis and Forecast" may describe areas of dense fog reducing visibility below 1 nautical mile, areas of significant structural icing, and expected conditions for the next 36 hours.

Example

High Seas Forecast: National Weather Service Washington DC/TPC Miami FL Marine Prediction Center/MFB *[Marine Forecast Branch]*. 1030 UTC *[1030 Universal Coordinated Time, equivalent to Z Time or Greenwich Mean Time; this is five hours ahead of U.S. East Coast Standard Time]* Sep 27 1997. Superseded by next issuance in 6 hours. *[Forecasts are produced every six hours, and older versions are invalidated by the issuance of a newer forecast.]* Securite: *[The term sécurité designates this message as important. It should be given immediate attention.]* North Atlantic north of 32N to 65N and west of 35W. Synopsis valid 0600 UTC Sep 27. Forecast valid *[valid time is the time this forecast is accurate]* 1800 UTC Sep 28. Warnings storm 48N 45W 984 MB will move NE 35 kt. Winds 35 to 50 kt and seas 15 to 25 ft within 360 NM S quadrant. *[Strong systems are often divided in quadrants (quarters) when winds and seas are significantly different in sections of a single system.]* Winds 25 to 40 kt and seas 10 to 18 ft elsewhere within 600 NM SE semicircle and 300 NM NW semicircle. Forecast storm *["forecast storm" indicates where the storm will be in next 24 hours]* well E of forecast waters. Forecast winds 25 to 35 kt and seas 8 to 16 ft N of 57N and E of 44W. Gale 65N 37W 988 MB nearly stationary. Winds 25 to 40 kt and seas 12 to 22 ft N of 59N and E of 44W. Forecast gale absorbed in circulation of forecast storm mentioned above. *[It is important to watch systems outside your immediate area, as they often affect local conditions. Here the gale is forecast to be absorbed by a storm.]* Forecast gale 45N 42W 1002 MB. Forecast winds 25 to 35 kt and seas 8 to 15 ft within 420 NM W semicircle. Synopsis and forecast high 44N 79W 1020 MB will move E 20 kt. Forecast high 43N 60W 1023 MB. N Atlantic N of 3N to 32N W of 35W including Caribbean Sea and Gulf of Mexico.

Synopsis and forecast Atlc synopsis at 0600 UTC Sep 27, ridge high pressure 32N40W to 27N70W. *[A ridge is an elongated area of high pressure, and the coordinates given here denote the endpoints of this ridge.]* Stationary front 32N75W to 1007 MB low near 28N83W. Forecast by 1800 UTC Sep 28 little change to ridge. Low hours N. Atlc at 0600 UTC Sep 27 from 12N to 23N E of 55W winds E to 20 kt and seas to 8 ft in E swell. Forecast through 1800 UTC Sep 28 between 10N and 20N E of 50W winds 20 kt seas 8 ft associated with a tropical wave. *[Tropical waves, areas of low pressure in tropical regions, are sources of tropical depressions, storms, and hurricanes.]* Atlc at 0600 UTC Sep 27 W of 70W winds SE to S to 20 kt and seas to 8 ft. Forecast at 1800 UTC Sep 28 little change. Atlc at 0600 UTC Sep 27 N of 30N between 58W and 65W winds SW 20 kt and seas to 8 ft. Forecast at 1800 UTC Sep 28 N of 30N and E of 50W winds SW to 20 kt and seas to 8 ft. Remainder Atlc winds less than 20 kt and seas less than 8 ft through 1800 UTC Sep 28.

Caribbean synopsis at 0600 UTC Sep 27 trough *[elongated area of low pressure]* extreme NW section will gradually weaken. By 0600 UTC Sep 28 trough dissipated. Caribbean at 0600 UTC Sep 27 from 11N to 17N between 68W and 80W winds E to SE to 20 kt and seas to 8 ft. N of 15N W of 80W winds SE to S 20 kt and seas to 8 ft remainder Caribbean winds less than 20 kt and seas less than 8 ft through 1800 UTC Sep 28. Gulf of Mexico synopsis at 0600 UTC Sep 27 low pres 1007 MB *[1007 mb is the low's central pressure. Remember that 1013 mb is a normal sea-level pressure.]* 29N83W trailing front to 18N93W. Forecast at 1800 UTC Sep 28 low pres inland and front dissipated *[the low pressure will move inland and dissipate]* at 0600 UTC Sep 27 within 180 NM E semicircle of low pres and elsewhere N of 28N E of front winds SW to 20 kt with seas below 8 ft. N of 25N W of front winds NW to N to 20 kt *[note the wind shift from SW to NW across the front]* and seas less than 8 ft. Forecast at 1800 UTC Sep 28 N of 27N E of 87W winds SW to W to 20 kt and seas less than 8 ft. Remainder Gulf of Mexico winds less than 20 kt and seas below 8 ft through 1800 UTC *[1800 UTC is 5 hours earlier, making this forecast valid at 1300 East Coast Time.]* Sep 28.

TROPICAL WEATHER DISCUSSION

Tropical weather discussions provide detailed descriptions and narratives of tropical weather features, not forecasts or analyses. They are insights into the whys and hows of specific weather features and patterns. Discussions make use of satellite imagery, observations, modeling, and meteorologists' expert opinions.

These discussions will mention upper-level troughs and ridges that should appear on a 500-mb chart for the same time and area. Height contour changes at 500 mb signify intensification or dissipation of surface systems. Increasing heights over a ridge indicate a strengthening surface high-pressure center, while decreasing heights over a trough indicate a strengthening surface low-pressure system, and vice versa.

A *blocking ridge* is a strong high-pressure region that is "blocking" the normal west-to-east flow of weather systems. The *jet axis* is where the strongest 500-mb winds are found. Latitude and longitude coordinates are provided for all features so that the recipient may index the broadcast with charts, imagery, and text information.

Cyclonic refers to counterclockwise rotation in the Northern Hemisphere, and a trough that is increasing in strength by growing in a north–south direction is said to be *digging*. Abbreviations are often used with regard to specific weather models, such as AVN, NGM, RUC, ETA, and others (see chapter 2). Knowing specifics of these models, though helpful, is not necessary.

Convection refers to vertical motion and is associated with low-pressure areas and cloud formation. *Subsidence* describes descending air and thus occurs in areas of high pressure and clear skies. When a system or feature is *embedded*, it is "stuck" within another system and will move accordingly.

Tropical waves are areas of low pressure within or near the ITCZ (see chapter 1). They usually feature extensive cloud development accompanied by showers and thunderstorms. Tropical waves originate in the eastern Atlantic and move west following tradewind flow.

Strong local effects are often mentioned, such as gale- and storm-force winds that result from air being funneled through mountain gaps and around prominent landmasses. In the example below, this occurs in the Gulf of Tehuantepec.

Our example gives an update on tropical storm Grace, including its position, direction of movement, forecast position, and extended outlook. Note the warning concerning possible errors in the forecast position. Satellite imagery is crucial for monitoring powerful systems such as Grace, because the models are often unable to keep up with the system's rapid and seemingly erratic movement.

Example

Tropical Weather Discussion: Tropical Analysis and Forecast Branch Tropical Prediction Center Miami FL 805 AM EDT Sat Sep 27 1997. Tropical Weather Discussion for: North America Central America, Gulf of Mexico Caribbean Sea and Atlantic Ocean to the African coast from 32N to the equator excluding continental South America. The following information is based on satellite imagery weather observations and meteorological analysis. Based on 0600 UTC surface analysis and 1015 UTC satellite imagery. *[Satellite imagery— including infrared, visible, and water vapor—is blended with observations and computer analysis to arrive at a blended product called a "discussion."]*

Tropical cyclones, none. Deep synoptic weather features:

Hemispheric long wave *[Long waves are upper-level troughs, the features that support short-wave troughs, which in turn support surface low-pressure development]* pattern remains in a four wave configuration *[four troughs and four ridges]*. This has been the rule for the past several weeks. During the past several days the Western Hemisphere long waves *[upper-level troughs]* have been most active taking on strong almost winter like intensity. And lodged between these two strong troughs has been an equally active and strong blocking ridge *[an upper-level ridge, which blocks west-to-east flow of weather features]* located over the northwestern part of the American continent. In the past 24 hr this unusually strong pattern has begun to relax. While the two Western Hemisphere troughs

remain fairly strong there has been a 30-meter height rise at the 500-mb level during this period *[indicates high pressure is building beneath upper-level ridge]*. The main change taking place during this period has been the weakening of the blocking ridge over the NW. This feature has opened up and is shifting east to the mid portion of the continent.

The strong N Atlantic trough's main axis is along 50W and is N of 40N. There persists a weakness oriented NE/SW over the Ohio Valley that appears to extend S to the N Gulf Coast. There are indications this feature is weakening further.

Over the subtropics, high pressure is reasserting itself as the two Western Hemisphere troughs weaken. During the past 48 hr the Atlantic long wave ridge *[extended area of high pressure]* has shifted east and strengthened slightly. Tonight's position is over the mid Atlantic near 30N50W with an increase in heights of 20 meters at 500 mb during the past 24 hr. Three deep layer features: The ridge W of 100W over the eastern portion of the continent intensifies with height. A broad trough over the eastern portion of the continent and NW Atlantic is the second deep layer feature. The trough is mainly N of 35N but a low level center is located over the lower Mississippi Valley and is associated with features in the mid and upper levels. The third feature is the Atlantic ridge *[elongated area of high-pressure]* with its customary orientation of west to east along 27N over the western and central Atlantic and then extending NE over the eastern Atlantic. This eastern portion is the best identified deep layer feature whereas the western and central portions of the upper ridge have an embedded trough *[the embedded trough indicates an area of low pressure that is well developed and supported]* oriented NE/SW from near 35N40W to 20N70W with a closed center near 25N63W. Low levels, a surface 1024 mb high is located near 32N35W and has a ridge axis along 29N40W 27N60W to 24N80W *[the coordinates of the ridge; connecting these points will show the surface position of high pressure]*. A stationary front extended from 32N75W west and SW to N Florida where a weak frontal low 1007 mb was near 28N83W. The front continued SW to near 23N90W as a weak cold front. Middle levels, a closed cyclonic center over the lower Miss Valley is the strongest feature. This system is moving slowly east according to the AVN MDL *[an aviation computer model]* but may be a little N of E according to the latest SAT pictures. Much weaker cyclonic rotation located near 19N86W according to the AVN. This feature is hard to discern under the upper ridge over the area and the copious cloud cover. Another weak vortex *["vortex" refers to an area of circular flow, often measured in terms of vorticity]* is over the NE Caribbean extending SW over Puerto Rico and the Dominican Republic. The AVN is projecting a new center forming over the central Caribbean and this looks reasonable in the water vapor *[water vapor imagery comes from geostationary GOES imagery, where extent of water vapor represents energy within the atmosphere]* where the best cyclonic rotation is in this area.

High levels, sharp upper ridge NE/SW from 37N100W to Central Baja appears to be shifting east slowly N of 30N. Ridge has good digging northerly flow over OK/E TX *[Oklahoma and east Texas]* turning more NE over northern Mexico. Flow is on the backside of the well-defined upper trough that extends from a strong center near 33N87W SW to just S of Brownsville and NE Mexico. Very dry sinking air in trough working S over the western Gulf beginning to feel the fringe moisture from the E Pacific tropical storm Olaf *[Moisture from tropical systems can fuel the development of low-pressure systems days and weeks after the tropical system has diminished.]* Upper ridge over Central America NE across Cuba and the western Bahamas to 30N78W. Ridge contaminated with clouds from considerable convection *[upward airflow causing condensation—clouds]*.

Weak cyclonic *[counterclockwise]* rotation near 28N55W almost stationary. Another of about the same strength near 23N39W also moving little. Both embedded in a large upper ridge that covers the mid Atlantic N of 20N. Over the tropics along 10N a persistent westerly flow of 20 to 30 kt works its way from 70W east to 35W where it accelerates NE to 20N20W. The westerly flow is evident over West Africa, being accelerated by a strong upper trough N of 25N along 10W.

Tropical waves/tropical lows, tropical wave aloft *[an upper-level area of low pressure that will support surface low development]* along 18N71W 15N73W 10N74W at 27/0000 UTC now along 74W/75W S of 18N. It is moving W at 10–15 knots. Isolated moderate convection *[indicating rain, showers, and thunderstorms]* is within 120 nm of 76W from 10N–15N. Tropical wave *[area of low pressure]* along 20N56W 15N58W 7N58W at 27/0000 UTC now along 59W/60W S of 21N. It is moving W 15–20 kt. Widely scattered moderate to isolated strong convection is within 120 NM of 16N53W 22N58W 21N62W. Widely scattered showers are within 120 nm of 12N62W 18N62W 22N64W.

Tropical wave previously along 42W/43W at 27/0000 UTC now along 43W/44W S of 12N. It is moving W 15–20 kt. Caribbean Sea scattered moderate to strong convection is along S coast of Cuba within 90 NM of 21N between 81W–86W. Scattered moderate to isolated strong convection is in W Caribbean along coast of Central America within 60 nm of 20N84W 15N84W 10N83W. Scattered moderate convection is over Lake Maracaibo *[located at 10 north/72 west; it is necessary to have an appropriate chart of the area]* within 90 nm of 11N72W 7N71W. Widely scattered moderate convection is over Hispaniola within 60 nm of 20N74W 18N69W.

Atlantic Ocean, numerous strong convection is in W Atlc within 90 nm of 31N81W32N74W. In addition scattered moderate to isolated strong convection is in W Atlc within 90 nm of 29N81W 29N76W 31N72W. Similar activity is N of Dominican Republic within 90 nm of 21N70W 23N65W. Scattered moderate convection is in central Atlc within 60 nm of 24N36W 28N41W in association with upper low. ITCZ *[the Intertropical Convergence Zone, or Doldrums]* axis of ITCZ-related clouds/convection centered along 5N11W 9N20W11N35W 12N48W 11N60W. Scattered moderate to isolated strong convection exists S of ITCZ within 60 nm of 4N27W 6N33W. Widely scattered moderate to isolated strong convection is from 6N–14N between 14W–25W. Scattered moderate convection is within 60 nm of axis E of 15W. Widely scattered moderate convection is within 60 nm of axis between 25W–30W. *[When satellite imagery is viewed in conjunction with this discussion, a very detailed and accurate assessment of present and future conditions emerges.]*

TROPICAL WEATHER OUTLOOK

Tropical weather outlooks give a brief overview of tropical weather, providing information on significant features and mentioning any possible storm or hurricane development. Tropical waves are areas of low pressure easily tracked on satellite imagery. A cooling cloud top on a tropical wave indicates an increase in its height, a likely sign of a strengthening system, and a tropical wave's appearance on VIS imagery as bright white indicates a dense cloud, filled with moisture.

Example

Tropical Weather Outlook: Tropical Weather Outlook National Weather Service Miami FL 1130 AM EST Fri Nov 20 1998 for the North Atlantic, Caribbean Sea and the Gulf of Mexico, tropical storm formation is not expected through Saturday. *[These are brief messages but very useful in determining the presence and likelihood of tropical weather features, especially storms and hurricanes.]*

4

Surface Charts

Weather charts are the backbone of weather analysis and forecasts. They put the weather in motion for us, showing synoptic features and specific conditions in a variety of formats and for a range of geographic areas. Weather charts enable us to see local conditions in relation to larger weather systems, providing an overall view of the weather and permitting accurate forecasts. Charts, for example, are produced for surface, sea-state, upper-air, and oceanographic conditions. There are charts produced specifically for marine use as well as for aircraft, balloons, firefighting, emergency response, agriculture, and other applications. Regardless of their application, charts are produced in two formats, analysis and forecast, described in chapter 1. Analyses provide a snapshot of conditions at a specific time. Forecast charts show how the weather should look at a future time, based upon extrapolation from current conditions. Forecasts are routinely prepared out to 144 hours, and further if needed. Accuracy diminishes the farther out a forecast is run, with four days presently being the maximum length without losing too much accuracy.

ANALYSIS AND FORECAST CHARTS

National Weather Service meteorologists produce four detailed surface analysis charts each day, depicting isobars, winds, frontal systems (occluded, stationary, cold, and warm), low- and high-pressure center positions and central pressures.

Warnings for gale- and storm-force systems are labeled and spelled out in bold capital letters. For tropical cyclone activity an appropriate symbol is marked next to the disturbance: a circle with a dot inside represents a tropical disturbance, a circle with an X inside a tropical depression, a circle with open center and spiraling arms a tropical storm, and a circle with a filled center and spiraling arms a hurricane or typhoon.

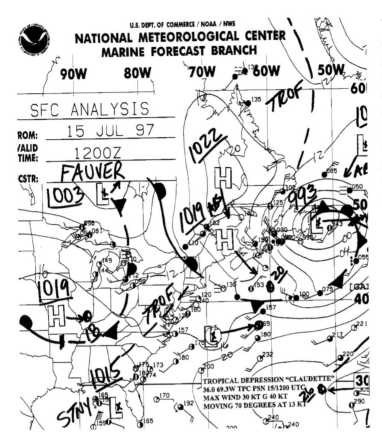

Top: *Surface analysis for 15 July 1997 shows tropical depression Claudette in position 36.0 north and 69.3 west with winds at 30 knots gusting to 40 knots. The system is moving in a direction of 070 T at a speed of 13 knots. Notice that this position is given in UTC (Universal Time Coordinated) time. A surface trough of low pressure lies over the U.S. East Coast, and the Atlantic high pressure is strong with a central pressure of 1031 mb.*

Bottom: *This 24-hour forecast shows classic low-pressure formation along the U.S. East Coast. Note two low-pressure systems developing to gale force along the cold front. A large surface ridge (represented by the saw-tooth pattern) and a high-pressure center of 1019 mb lie along 65 west longitude. Notice the fog (horizontal dashes) on the back (west) side of lows. These lows will track north along the ridge, following a typical East Coast autumn route toward Nova Scotia, bringing northeasters to the coast of New England.*

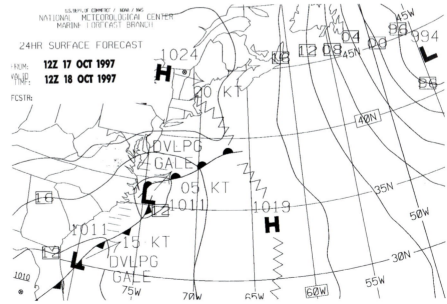

WXMAP GRAPHICS REFERENCE CHART

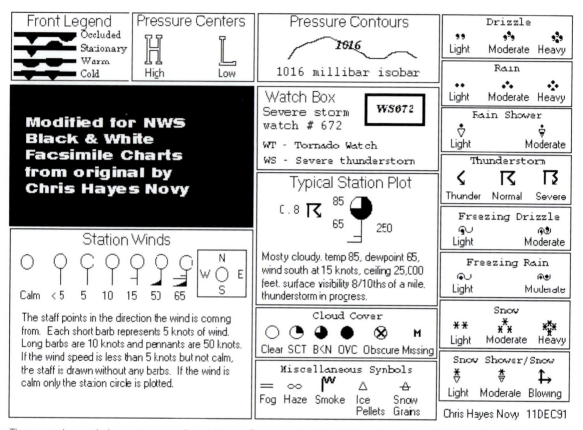

These are the symbols most commonly used on surface analysis and forecast charts to denote weather features. Although not shown here, surface pressure is often included with station plots, which are placed on the upper right of the wind symbols.

Each surface analysis depicts the 24-hour forecast position for each low- and high-pressure system. Pressure decreases of 24 mb or more in any given 24-hour period are noted in bold capital letters as "RAPIDLY INTENSIFYING." If a low-pressure system is forecast to become a gale or storm, then "DVLPG GALE" OR "DVLPG STORM" is written near the "L" which denotes the low-pressure system.

Surface forecasts are produced using a blending of information obtained from forecast models and personal experience and are generated at 00Z, 06Z, 12Z, and 18Z, with isobar spacing done at 4-mb intervals and labeled every 8 mb. The central pressures of highs and lows are labeled with three or four digits, placed near the appropriate L or H, and underlined. The locations of cold fronts, warm fronts, occluded and stationary fronts, troughs, and ridges are also noted. Meteorologists locate surface features using a variety of indicators: temperature differences; wind direction, speed, and changes over time; humidity and dew point; pressure at specific locations and pressure differences; cloud types and cloud cover; and associated upper-level features.

Surface winds reported from buoys and ships

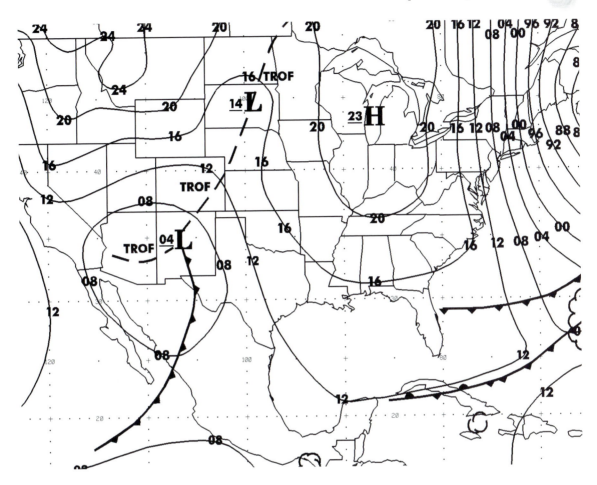

This North American Surface Analysis Chart for 2 December shows a large low-pressure system over New Mexico, with a cold front and two troughs extending from its center. There is an area of high pressure over the Great Lakes with a central pressure of 1023 mb. Isobar lines are marked with only the last two digits (the implicit 9 or 10 is not shown). There exists a strong low to the east, indicated by tight isobars, of which only the west side is shown. Winds in New England on this day were northerly and brisk.

are also shown with wind direction (on an eight-point compass rose) and speed, as well as cloud cover and barometric pressure. Pressure is coded using three digits, with the rightmost digit being tenths and the implicit 9 or 10 not shown.

Surface analysis charts for ocean regions are issued in two parts which overlap by 10 degrees of longitude, between 165 and 175 west in the Pacific Ocean and between 40 and 50 west in the Atlantic Ocean. Both charts show low and high pressure location by drawing an arrow to the 24-hour position, labeled with an "X" for lows and a circle with "X" inside for highs.

The reason for issuing surface analysis charts in two parts and in a larger format than other weather charts is to allow their use as a plotting sheet. (Surface charts are drawn in a mercator projection, allowing course lines and measurements to

(continued on page 50)

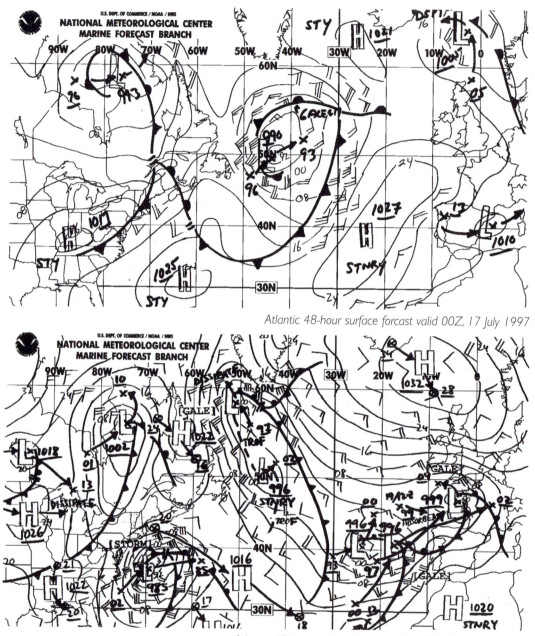

Atlantic 48-hour surface forcast valid 00Z, 17 July 1997

Atlantic 48-hour surface forecast valid 12Z, 20 October 1997

These four surface charts show 48-hour forecasts for Atlantic and Pacific waters, with the three Atlantic charts allowing a seasonal comparison. An X represents a low, and a circled X represents a high. The letter (L or H) shows the position of the system at the "valid time"

noted on charts (not shown here). As is standard practice, the X preceding the L or H (indicated by arrows) marks the position of the system 24 hours prior to valid time; the X following marks its position 24 hours after valid time. Notice how fronts attached to lows connect

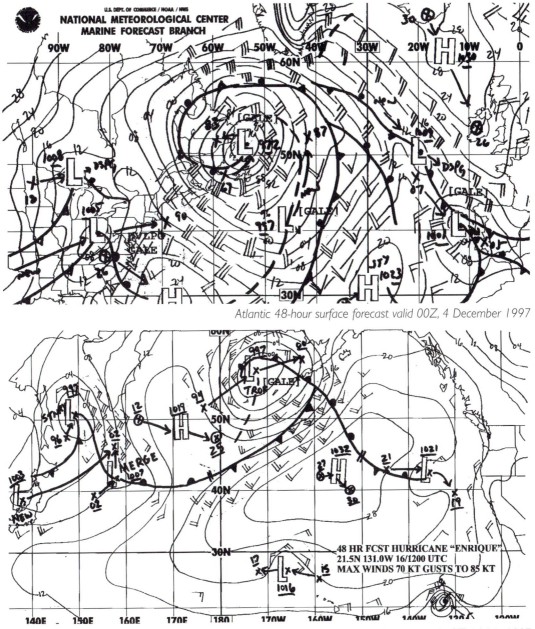

Atlantic 48-hour surface forecast valid 00Z, 4 December 1997

Pacific 48-hour surface forecast valid 12Z, 16 July 1997

with other lows, showing flow and continuity between weather systems. Double-hatched lines seen on fronts indicate a discontinuity, where a front may change from cold to warm, or to stationary or occluded. Locate trough lines behind cold fronts and new lows forming along troughs. Hurricane Enrique is shown on the Pacific chart, a compact system compared to the large gale over the Aleutians. Compare the charts for July with that for December; in particular notice the differences in strength and location of the low-pressure systems.

be drawn and read directly off the chart. Additionally, surface charts are produced using a small-scale–large-area format so weather features are easily read and track lines easily plotted.) A surface chart and 500-mb chart read together permit tracking the direction and intensity of surface lows, highs, and fronts, as we will see in chapter 8. As mentioned earlier, surface analysis charts show the atmosphere at a moment in time and as such should be compared with other prediction products, such as satellite imagery and long-range predictions, to detect and verify changes that may have occurred after the analysis was completed.

HOW TO GET THESE CHARTS

To improve access to weather charts the National Weather Service maintains a homepage on the Internet where all weather charts produced and otherwise transmitted are now available. These addresses are listed in appendix 3. Charts are compressed in formats known as TIFF and GIF and require a viewer software program to be opened and used. Details on chart viewers are provided at the National Weather Services homepage on the Internet, as well as information on obtaining charts and weather data via satellite, radio broadcasts, and other electronic means. (See appendix 3 for detailed listings.)

MEASURING AND REPRESENTING WIND SPEED AND DIRECTION

Wind is the horizontal movement of air, with speed most often measured in knots and direction

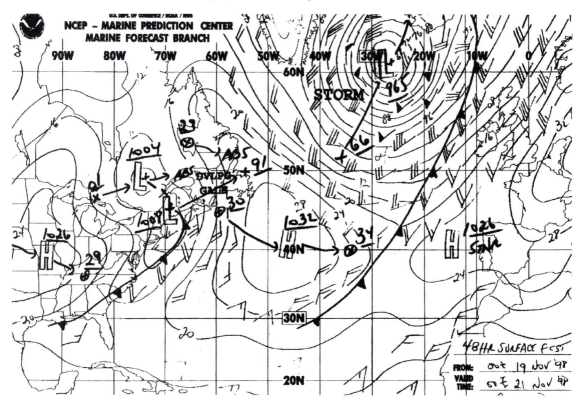

This 48-hour surface forecast chart shows wind arrows representing predicted wind speed and direction at 00Z on 21 November 1998 based upon data collected at 00Z on 19 November 1998.

in degrees true. Actual and predicted wind speed and direction are shown on weather maps using arrows pointing in the direction the wind is blowing, with tail feathers denoting speed in 5-knot increments. Wind speed is shown on analysis charts using wind arrows surrounded by additional data such as barometric pressure, air temperature, and cloud cover. Forecast charts use wind arrows, showing wind speed and direction, but have no accompanying data.

A given wind speed and direction is actually a mean value measured or expected over a 10-minute period. A mean value is used since winds oscillate and instantaneous readings are often misleading.

Increases in speed are called *gusts* and decreases, *lulls*. Prolonged gusts, when wind speed increases by at least 15 knots, are called *squalls*. Squalls are most often associated with rapidly developing and moving weather events that are often not shown on synoptic weather charts. The charts do, however, show the weather systems that support these events, such as a cold front that spawns the squalls.

Weather forecast charts provide wind information representative of large-scale (synoptic) weather conditions. Most weather models—computer simulations of forthcoming weather—are highly accurate in describing overall weather events, but are not designed to describe the specifics of local weather. When using synoptic forecasts, one must often factor in the effects of regional topography, ocean currents, and temperature differences.

On page 53 we discuss an example of local conditions significantly modifying the overall weather picture: Along the California coast, a thermal trough and Pacific high pressure often combine to produce

winds of greater strength than are normally predicted or expected.

HIGH PRESSURE

High-pressure areas exist where air descending from the upper atmosphere meets the Earth's surface and moves outward. High-pressure systems can bring warm or cold temperatures, depending upon where they form. But they always bring clear weather because of their low humidity, which minimizes cloud formation.

High-pressure systems are viewed warily by sailors, since they often bring light winds or calms. There is, however, a band of dependable winds near a high's perimeter. These dependable winds are found within a pressure gradient indicated by tight surface isobar lines and 500-mb contour lines.

There is always a strong gradient near a high's perimeter because, as air moves out from a high's center, its motion changes from *convective* (vertical) to *advective* (horizontal). An easy way to visualize the location of this pressure gradient is to examine a high in cross-section. Where the sides of a high-pressure mound are steep and isobars

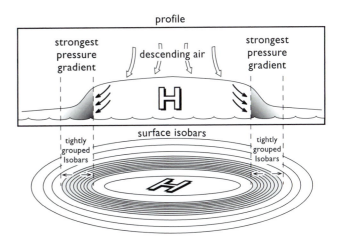

Dependable winds in a high-pressure system are found where isobars are close together. This occurs near the edges of high-pressure where pressure gradients are the steepest.

are close together, winds are consistent and well developed.

Satellite imagery, both infrared and visible, assists in locating high-pressure areas. High-pressure centers appear cloud-free and show warm surface temperatures. There are clouds, though, along a high's perimeter, where wind is found. Perimeter clouds that align themselves with wind flow, called cloud streets, indicate strong winds, as do distinct and well-defined individual clouds.

On 500-mb upper-air charts, strong surface winds are found beneath well-formed upper-level ridges. Tight and parallel 500-mb contour lines support well-developed surface winds, with surface wind speed averaging 30 to 50 percent of upper-level winds. For example, a 50-knot upper-level wind is reflected in 15- to 25-knot surface winds.

Sailing vessels wishing to use high-pressure systems to advantage must find this band of strong winds and then stay within its borders. Several strategies are used to accomplish this, depending on boat speed and movement of weather systems. Fast boats can catch and sail through high-pressure systems, whereas weather systems move over a slower boat's path. If a high is coming from behind, then a course change is necessary before the high arrives to ensure optimal use of the wind flow. If a high is stationary, then a course optimizing wind speed and direction must be determined as the systems are approached. Remember, in the Northern Hemisphere, high-pressure systems rotate clockwise, and in the Southern Hemisphere, counterclockwise, so courses need to be planned accordingly.

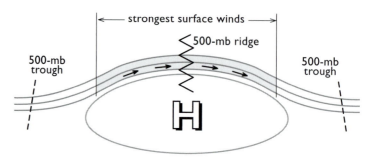

An accurate recording barometer and satellite imagery are the most important instruments for locating and then staying within a high's wind flow and are most effective used in conjunction with surface and upper-air 500-mb charts. Here, the strongest surface winds are along the 500-mb ridge.

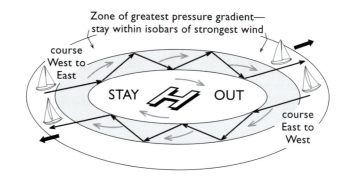

Keep your boat inside the narrow zone of greatest pressure gradient or within the isobars of strongest wind.

A barometer is the most important instrument for locating and then staying within a high's wind flow. If a high is overtaking a vessel, then a course change is necessary before the high arrives to ensure optimal use of the wind flow. A recording barometer, preferably one that continuously displays readings, is the most useful. There are several manufacturers of reliable electronic barometers that display pressure on a computer screen, enabling accurate monitoring of location within a high's wind flow.

Northeast and southeast tradewinds in the

Atlantic and Pacific Oceans come from the semi-permanent highs existing over those waters. These highs (the Pacific High and the Bermuda-Azores High) normally exist as a single system but often are split by intruding cold fronts attached to more northerly low-pressure systems. When a strong cold front approaches a high, it often splits the high's center in two. When this occurs, it is often possible to sail through what was the middle of the original high without losing wind.

THERMAL TROUGHS

Land and water handle heat input very differently: water absorbs heat with little change in temperature, whereas land temperature increases noticeably and quickly. When land is heated, its temperature goes up and it radiates heat back out to the air above. This causes the air overhead to rise. As air rises, additional air is drawn in to fill the void; this process creates a *thermal trough*. Sea breezes, which develop along beaches each day during the summer (usually first felt between 10 and 11 A.M. and strongest between 3 and 5 P.M.), are an example of thermal troughs: air rises above the land, and cooler ocean air moves landward to fill the void. Over California, thermal troughs develop in the spring and summer, as the sun's energy is concentrated into the Northern Hemisphere along 23 north latitude. As California's surface temperature rises, air above the land is warmed and rises, drawing in cooler air from the Pacific Ocean. In the height of summer, when temperatures over the land approach 90°F, there often develops a thermal trough so strong that it produces localized winds of 30 to 40 knots, and sometimes higher. Examine the accompanying surface

analysis chart for 18 May 1998 and note the trough (bold dashed line) over California, with tight isobar lines and 20- to 30-knot winds along the northern coast. These thermal winds are encouraged by the Pacific High (1033 mb), which is shown slowly sliding east. Thermal troughs are localized weather features not always reflected on synoptic (large-area and large-feature) charts. An early-morning chart might not show the strong winds that will develop as temperatures rise during a day. Watch for thermal troughs along coasts, especially wherever there are noticeable land-sea temperature differences. Thermal trough winds are often felt 100 miles or more out at sea, and many miles inland. Along the California coast, the combination of a strong coastal thermal gradient and a semipermanent Pacific high produces strong northerly winds, often reaching 40 to 50 knots.

Wind speed and direction on weather charts are shown in conjunction with isobar lines—a

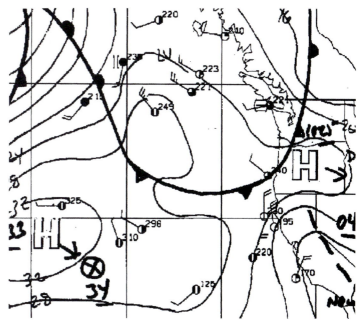

Thermal trough and Pacific high pressure combine to cause strong northerly winds along the California coast.

feature of all surface weather charts—which connect points of equal barometric pressure. Surface winds, in general, blow parallel to isobar lines, bending inward around low-pressure systems and outward around high-pressure systems. Closely spaced isobar lines indicate strong winds, and isobar lines with wide separation portend light winds.

GEOSTROPHIC WIND DIAGRAM

When wind speed is not shown on a chart, it can be calculated by measuring the perpendicular distance between isobar lines and using that value with a geostrophic wind diagram. Geostrophic (meaning Earth-driven) wind refers to the wind produced by the pressure gradient within a weather system combined with the deflecting force produced by the Earth's rotation, known as Coriolis force or effect (chapter 1). Two variables determine wind speed: distance between isobars, and the latitude of the location where wind speed is desired. First measure the perpendicular distance, or spacing, of isobar lines (in increments of 4 mb) in degrees of latitude. Then determine the latitude of the desired location and plug these two values into a geostrophic wind scale.

When identifying isobar lines, remember that normal sea-level pressure is 1013 mb and that the "thousands" and "hun-

dreds" units are often left out on isobar labels: for example, an isobar line representing 1016 mb would be labeled "16," and a pressure of 993 mb would be written as "93." The actual wind speed is less than the speed initially derived from a geostrophic wind scale due to friction between the wind and the underlying surface. In general, a speed of 60 to 70 percent of geostrophic wind speed is used for winds over water, and 50 percent is used for winds over land. (Friction over land is greater due to mountains, trees, buildings, etc.)

Wind speed on weather charts is calculated

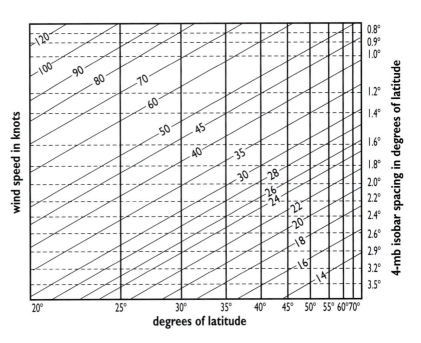

A geostrophic wind diagram. To determine geostrophic wind speed we would find the latitude of the desired location on the horizontal axis and follow that line up vertically; then we would plug in the isobar spacing (in degrees of latitude) on the vertical axis and follow that line horizontally. Wind speed is estimated according to the diagonals closest to the point of intersection. Remember to correct raw value for friction and temperature. This diagram is intended for use in the temperate latitudes. Isobar spacing that lends itself to geostrophic wind determination simply does not occur in tropical regions, where air masses are normally homogeneous.

Crossing the Doldrums from North to South Atlantic

Surface analysis charts provide pressure information that is useful in selecting a suitable crossing location. Where isobars spread apart there is likely to be little wind, so look for areas of tight pressure gradients. Take note of windless areas near Rio de Janeiro and along the African coast. The best crossing location is near where the North and South Atlantic permanent highs reach their point of closest approach.

Use a 500-mb chart to locate edges of high pressure and streamlines on a tropical chart (see chapter 6) to identify atmospheric disturbances and areas of convective activity; this is where you will find wind. Cross the Doldrums where cumulus clouds are broken, not too high, and trail off at an angle with increasing height. A sky covered with clouds indicates generally vertical motion with little downward flow, and thus little surface wind.

for a standard height of 10 meters (33.3 feet) above sea level. At heights below 33.3 feet, winds are normally less than shown on charts due to increased surface friction; above 33.3 feet, winds are normally greater.

It is often prudent to adjust geostrophic wind speed for the temperature difference between the underlying surface, whether water, land, or air. When cold air moves over warm water an unstable situation results, since cold air tends to sink and warm air sitting directly over warm water rises, bringing about convective (vertical) motion.

This convective motion produces gusty winds that are often 50 percent greater than calculated geostrophic winds. An air-water temperature difference of 10°C (approximately 20°F) or more is considered an unstable condition.

When warm air sits over cooler water a stable situation exists, since cold air will remain beneath the rising warm air, and a minimal amount of convection will occur. In this case a stable condition exists when the air-water temperature difference is 10°C (approximately 20°F) or more, with air warmer than water, and no adjustment to the geostrophic wind speed is necessary.

When winds associated with a developed low- and high-pressure system are stable they tend to blow more directly in toward the center of lows and out from the center of highs than

unstable winds, which tend to run parallel to isobar lines.

Unstable winds are most often found on the back side of cold fronts, where cold, dry arctic or polar air sweeps south over warm Atlantic and Pacific waters. Dense, cold air can produce formidable seas.

Additionally, sharp or noticeable bends in isobar lines have an effect on wind speed. As winds circle around low-pressure areas they spiral inward, but as these winds follow curves in isobar lines, centrifugal (outward) force counteracts their inward tendency. Therefore, around low-pressure systems winds tend to be diminished in areas where isobar lines make sharp or distinctive bends or turns, where outward and inward forces are counter to each other. Just the opposite occurs around high-pressure areas, where winds are blowing outward and centrifugal force accentuates this outward flow, increasing wind strength at turns or bends in isobar lines.

Meteorologists recommend adjusting wind speeds 20 percent up (around high pressure) or 20 percent down (around low pressure) to account for distinctive bends in isobar lines. Distinctive bends are most noticeable in the vicinity of warm and cold fronts, ridges, and troughs.

When winds blow contrary to a current or eddy, seas build quickly and to heights greater than would normally be expected. So watch for these conditions if operating near strong currents. When large wave conditions occur in the Gulf Stream, the National Weather Service broadcasts a "north wall bulletin" ("north wall" refers to the north or west edge of the Gulf Stream, where the strongest current usually flows and the largest seas often occur). Please refer to the examples in chapter 3.

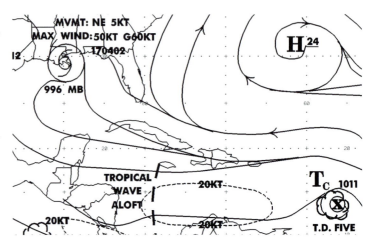

A portion of a tropical analysis chart shows several dominant features: a tropical storm going ashore near New Orleans with a central pressure of 996 mb; a tropical wave south of Cuba; tropical depression (TD) 5 with a central pressure of 1011 mb approaching the Caribbean's Windward Islands; and a large Atlantic high-pressure system. Note how the Atlantic high blocks northward movement of tropical waves and depressions.

BEAUFORT WIND SCALE

The Beaufort scale is routinely used in weather analysis and forecasts, so users should be able to convert Beaufort values to knots without hesitation.

The Beaufort scale		
BEAUFORT NUMBER	WIND SPEED (KNOTS)	SEA STATE
0	0	sea like a mirror
1	1–3	ripples like scales, no crests
2	4–6	small wavelets, crests glassy and not breaking
3	7–10	large wavelets, crests break, whitecaps begin
4	11–16	small waves, numerous whitecaps
5	17–21	moderate and longer waves; whitecaps and spray
6	22–27	larger waves, numerous whitecaps, much spray
7	28–33	sea heaps up, waves break, foam blows in streaks
8	34–40	moderate waves of greater length, foam blows in long streaks
9	41–47	high waves, rolling sea, dense streaks of foam, spray reduces visibility
10	48–55	very high waves, overhanging crests, sea white with foam, visibility reduced
11	56–63	exceptionally high waves, sea covered with foam, visibility poor
12	64+	waves tremendous, air filled with spray, sea white with foam, visibility nil

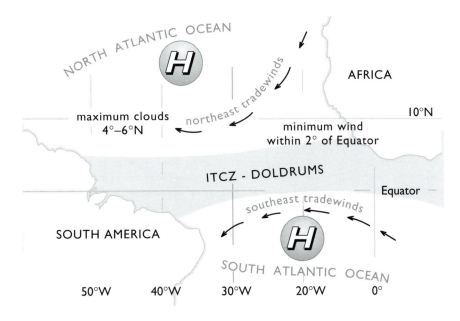

NORTH ATLANTIC OCEAN

H

AFRICA

northeast tradewinds

maximum clouds
4°–6°N

minimum wind
within 2° of Equator

10°N

ITCZ - DOLDRUMS

Equator

southeast tradewinds

SOUTH AMERICA

H

SOUTH ATLANTIC OCEAN

50°W   40°W   30°W   20°W   0°

Crossing the Doldrums. Light winds and rain showers are found near the equator in an area known as the Doldrums, or the Intertropical Convergence Zone (ITCZ). The location of the Doldrums changes with the season and is affected by the amount of heat being received from the sun, moving north during the Northern Hemisphere summer and south during the winter. The Doldrums can be found at any given time by locating the area where northeast and southeast tradewinds converge.

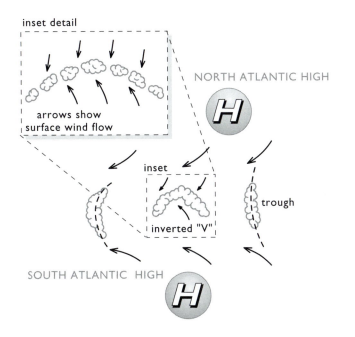

inset detail

arrows show
surface wind flow

NORTH ATLANTIC HIGH

H

inset

inverted "V"

trough

SOUTH ATLANTIC HIGH

H

Inverted V cloud shapes in the Doldrums. Southeast tradewinds entering the Doldrums often push northward with enough force to create a bubble or inverted V in the east-to-west surface air flow. These bubbles disturb the normal wind pattern, often producing overcast conditions and encouraging counterclockwise surface wind flow. With sufficient development, inverted Vs can become tropical waves, disturbances, storms, and even hurricanes.

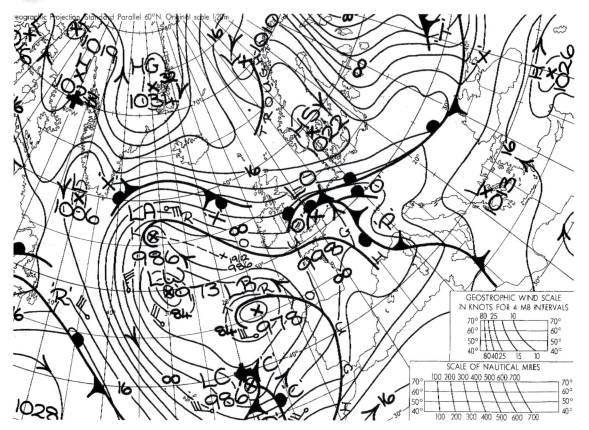

A British surface analysis chart for 20 December 1996 showing standard weather features: centers of highs and lows, fronts, isobars, and wind arrows. Notice the geostrophic wind diagram located at the bottom right. To use this type of diagram, measure the perpendicular distance between the 4-mb isobars with dividers and place one point of the dividers at the latitude value of the desired area on the left margin. Then lay out the dividers horizontally and estimate wind speed according to the speed curves closest to where the other point falls.

Also notice two areas of low pressure in close proximity to each other near the center of the chart. A trough of low pressure exists between these lows, as common isobar lines bind the centers. But the greatest area of instability probably lies along the dashed trough line just to the north. Look out, England!

Broken clouds indicate a mixture of convective (vertical) and advective (horizontal) motion and may signal the approach of tradewinds.

Radar (see appendix 1) is useful for identifying clouds, because water droplets are good reflectors. Dense clouds are likely to bring squalls and strong winds. Use satellite imagery to locate sea breezes, along the South American coast for example, by identifying lines of cumulus clouds.

Cloud-free areas are to be avoided, as they indicate little or no surface wind. Easterly waves, areas of low pressure moving from east to west across the Doldrums, are seen on satellite imagery as an inverted V cloud shape, with the apex pointing north. These Vs are most often seen between 5 and 25 degrees north latitude and have four-day separations. A 3-mb pressure drop and a shift in wind from northeast to southeast signal their

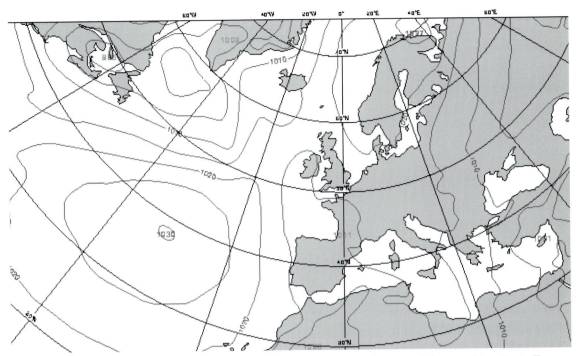

This surface analysis chart produced by the European Center for Medium Range Forecasting shows just isobars, providing a general picture of high- and low-pressure centers. Note the large 1030-mb Atlantic high pressure and the 995-mb low over Nova Scotia. These charts are used for general guidance and to build 6- to 10-day forecasts.

arrival. The duration of a wave is 36 to 48 hours, and winds often reach gale force for a brief period of time. Cold fronts, attached to midlatitude lows, often drop into the Doldrums and can bring a brief increase in wind speed. They can also disrupt and counteract Doldrums winds, producing areas of little or no wind near the bottom quarter of cold fronts. Once again, watch clouds, isobars, and sea-level pressure.

5

Upper-Air Charts and Jet Stream Systems

Upper-air weather charts show the strength and direction of upper-air winds, which influence the development and movement of surface troughs, ridges, lows, and highs. A full understanding of surface weather features, their development, and their movement is only gained when upper-level winds and features are considered and understood.

Each wave, or undulation, within the jet stream either moves cold air south or warm air north, causing mixing of air masses and formation of fronts. The extent of surface feature development depends on many factors, primary among them

- ◆ **amplitude** (latitude span) of upper-level troughs and ridges
- ◆ **length** (longitude span) of upper-level trough or ridge
- ◆ **wind speed** within troughs and ridges
- ◆ **geographic location** of troughs and ridges

TYPES OF UPPER-AIR CHARTS

There is an assortment of upper-air charts used in weather forecasting, each named for its elevation above sea level. Charts for various elevations show wind direction and speed at that particular pressure level and are used to determine various weather features. For example, information on precipitation (snow, rain, hail) is found by examining an 850-mb (5,000-ft) level chart, and airline pilots look at a 200-mb (39,000-ft) level chart to locate the strongest winds within the core of the jet stream.

Because the base of the jet stream is at 500 mb, wind at the 500-mb level controls the development and movement of surface weather features. Since sea-level pressure is 1013 mb, the 500-mb level is approximately halfway through the atmosphere (500 mb is about half of 1013 mb), giving it a midlatitude elevation of roughly 18,000 to 20,000 feet. For comparison, a pressure of 50 mb is found at 67,000 feet and 0 mb at 600 miles.

Winds at the 500-mb level, and generally throughout the jet stream, blow from west to east. Since there is little friction and disturbance from land topography at upper altitudes, jet stream winds follow an undulating path with north–south undulations superimposed on the eastward progress of alternating troughs and ridges. This pattern is monitored and mapped by National Weather Service (NWS) computer models and represented on charts. These charts are provided to users by radiofacsimile broadcasts and NWS Internet access.

Upper-air (500-mb) charts are produced in both analysis and forecast format. Analyses are generated twice each day at 00Z and 12Z. A 12-hour forecast is often produced along with an analysis, and a 48-hour forecast for both Atlantic and Pacific Oceans is also produced at 00Z and 12Z. Additionally, there are 60-hour (two-and-a-half-day) 500-mb forecasts available. Upper-air charts are produced in conjunction with surface charts with the same forecast period (12-, 48-, and 60-hour), so surface and 500-mb charts can be paired for comparison and corroboration of weather features.

Again, as upper-level winds move from west to east as ribbons of air, they also undulate in a north–south wave pattern. Dips are called *troughs*, and rises are called *ridges*, just as ocean waves have troughs and ridges. As we saw in chapter 1, in the Northern Hemisphere troughs flow with counterclockwise tendencies and ridges with clockwise tendencies. The direction of flow, or motion, is important because on the Earth's surface low-pressure systems (depressions, gales, storms) form under upper-level troughs, and high-pressure systems form under upper-level ridges. In the Northern Hemisphere, the counter-clockwise motion of upper-level troughs reinforces the counterclockwise tendency of surface lows. Upper-level ridges likewise reinforce the clockwise motion of surface highs. The opposite occurs in the Southern Hemisphere.

When a surface low forms under an upper-level trough, or a surface high under a ridge, it then moves in the direction of upper-level flow at a speed between one-third and one-half of upper-level wind speed. For example, if wind speed within a trough at the 500-mb level is 60 knots, then a surface low under this trough will move across the Earth's surface at a speed between 20 and 30 knots (between one-third and one-half of 60 knots).

Within a surface low or high, the greatest wind speed will be approximately 50 percent of the 500-mb wind above the system. So a surface low under 60 knots of 500-mb wind will develop 30 knots of internal wind, and as this low devel-

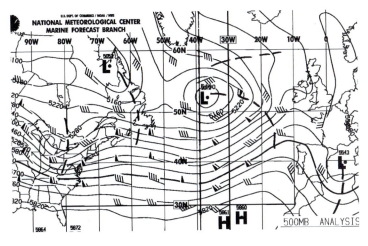

Five short wave troughs (dashed lines) represent areas of unsettled weather where surface low-pressure systems are likely to form. Jet stream flow across the mid-Atlantic in this case is called zonal since there is a minimum of north–south fluctuation in the jet stream. The 5,640-meter height contour, known as the storm track, is situated in this analysis along 35 north. This contour marks the area of greatest jet stream activity and the track generally followed by gales and storms.

ops it will move across the Earth's surface at a speed between 20 and 30 knots.

Since 500-mb troughs support the formation of surface lows, the National Weather Service marks the location of upper-level troughs with a dashed line. Surface troughs are also marked using the same dashed-line symbol, since troughs, whether located at upper levels or on the surface, are generally areas of instability and counterclockwise wind rotation (in the Northern Hemisphere). During hurricane season, upper-air flow patterns provide insight into tropical disturbance movement when these systems enter midlatitudes from the tropics.

Solid contour lines on 500-mb charts represent heights above sea level where a pressure of 500 mb is found. These heights are noted in meters, so a line labeled "5,820" indicates a height of 5,820 meters (19,206 feet) above the Earth's surface. On average, the 500-mb level is found around 18,000 feet. To put this altitude in perspective, consider that Mount Everest rises to 29,000 feet, bringing its climbers well into the jet stream flow as they approach the summit.

On every 500-mb chart the 5,640 height contour is shown in bold since its location, in a north–south orientation, marks both the storm track and the southern extent of Beaufort Force 7 (28- to 33-knot) or greater midlatitude surface winds in the winter, and Force 6 (22- to 27-knot) winds in summer. The 5,640 height in and of itself is not significant, but its location happens to mark the area where the most mixing of cold, dry air with warm, moist air occurs, and therefore an area of greatest low-pressure development. Generally, the 5,640 height contour lies

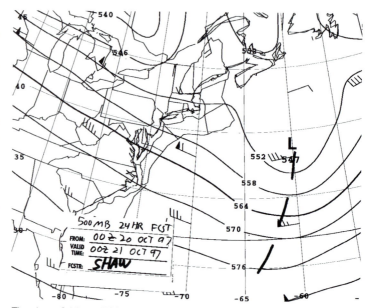

The three 24-hour 500-mb charts on these two pages show a variety of troughs and upper-air wind speeds. Note that the strongest winds on all charts lie near the 5,640 height contour, the storm track. The location of height contours (in terms of latitude) varies with season and the amount of warm and cold air influencing jet stream flow. Note how some troughs have pronounced amplitude while others are broader or flatter. Troughs with tight height contours and noticeable north–south development tend to produce strong surface low-pressure systems.

near 50 degrees north/south latitude in the summer and near 40 degrees north/south in the winter. The 5,640 line is routinely used in initial route planning and track modification on extended ocean passages, since it provides tremendous insight into surface weather patterns and development.

Arrows on a 500-mb chart are drawn in 5- and 10-knot increments to show wind speeds greater than 30 knots. Areas where no wind arrows are drawn indicate winds less than 30 knots and variable in direction. Winds above 50 knots represent core jet stream winds and are drawn with a solid triangular flag symbol. When jet stream winds within an area of troughing approach or exceed 100 knots, a strong potential exists for rapidly developing low formation at the surface.

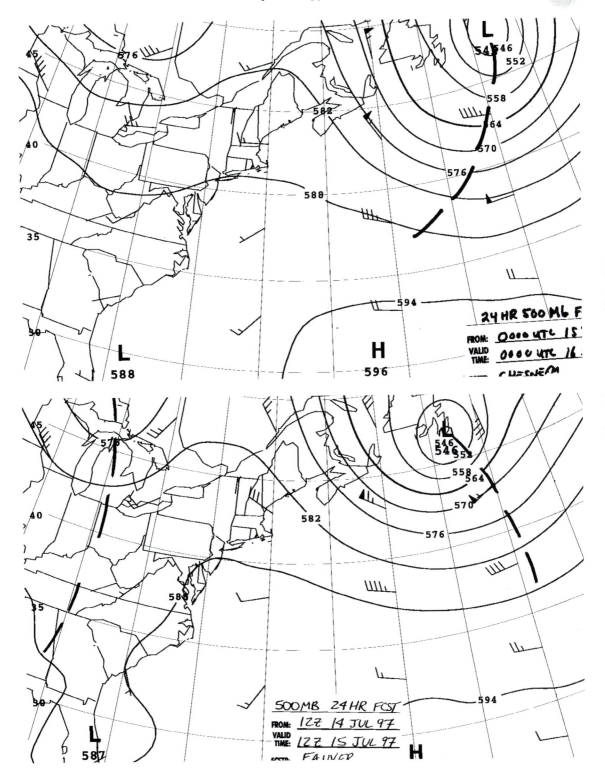

24 HR 500 MB F
FROM: 0000 UTC 15
VALID TIME: 0000 UTC 16
CHESNER

500MB 24HR FCST
FROM: 12Z 14 JUL 97
VALID TIME: 12Z 15 JUL 97
FCST. FAINCD

RAPIDLY INTENSIFYING LOWS

Rapidly developing lows tend to occur in a matter of hours over warm underlying surfaces, such as the Gulf Stream in the Atlantic Ocean and Kuroshio Current in the Pacific Ocean. Also called *meteorological bombs*, these systems develop from initial mild disturbances to full-strength storms in 12 to 24 hours.

Fortunately, 500-mb charts give indications of the potential for a rapidly intensifying low. One of these indications, as mentioned above, is the presence of 100-knot winds in a 500-mb trough.

Other indicators are

◆ An upper-level trough lying over warm ocean current.

◆ A trough showing enhanced north–south development, which leads to mixing of warm and cold air.

◆ The time of year is early fall or late winter, when temperature differences (gradients) within the atmosphere are greatest.

Numerous satellite images and charts showing low-pressure development are found in chapter 8.

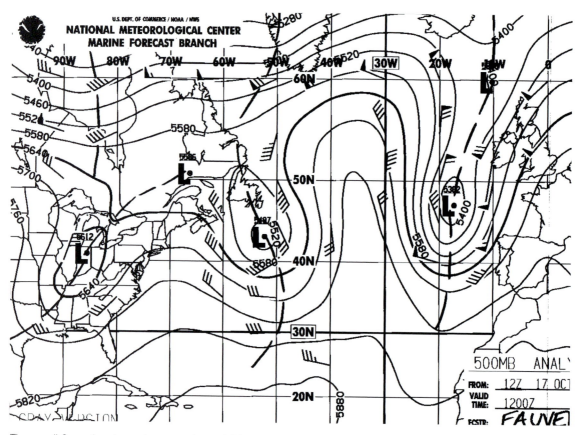

Three well-formed and prominent troughs and ridges across the midlatitudes show how support is provided for alternating low- and high-pressure systems. A trough is also noted over Greenland. A strong ridge near 35W resembles the shape of the Greek letter omega (Ω) and is called, appropriately, an omega block. Strong surface highs normally exist under omega blocks, forcing approaching low-pressure systems to move north or become stationary on the west side of the block.

Visual indicators of a rapidly developing low are the thickening and lowering of clouds, increase in swell height, and decrease in period. However, the clearest signal of the formation of these systems is a barometric pressure drop of 1 mb per hour for 12 consecutive hours.

OMEGA BLOCKS

Surface high-pressure systems are also located and analyzed using 500-mb charts. Strong surface highs frequently occur under strong upper-level ridges called *omega blocks*. The term *omega* comes from the path taken by upper-level wind, which resembles the Greek letter omega (Ω), and "blocks" refers to the fact that these systems block or deflect the movement of low-pressure systems approaching from the west, or upwind. An area of high pressure under an omega block normally has a central pressure of 1035 mb, which often develops to 1045 mb or greater. A description of high-pressure systems as seen on surface charts is found in chapter 4; sample satellite images of high-pressure blocks are found in chapter 8.

6

Specialty Charts

STREAMLINE CHARTS

Wind flow in tropical regions, 20 degrees north to 20 degrees south, is shown on weather charts using a format called *streamlines*. Streamlines are continuous lines showing wind direction resulting from tradewind convergence near the equator, also known as the Intertropical Convergence Zone (ITCZ).

Outside the tropics, wind flow is shown by isobar lines, with tight isobar lines indicating a significant pressure difference (gradient) and strong winds. However, since tropical regions do not have distinctive air masses and there is little mixing of warm and cold air masses, isobar lines are inadequate for representing tropical wind flow.

Convergence and rising air in tropical regions is caused by the abundance of heat pumped into tropical regions by the sun. This horizontal convergence and ascending air results in cumulus and cumulonimbus cloud development, which is tracked by weather satellites and used to determine wind speed and direction.

Tropical clouds have individual diameters of 1 to 50 miles and when clustered may have diameters from 50 to 500 miles. Cloud cells and clusters, however, are not consistent or continuous in their development, a result of uneven equatorial heating due to seasonal, geographic, and climatological variables.

Thus, there are noticeable fluctuations in tropical winds and weather, with transitions from calm to squalls and showers, followed by clear skies and sun, often occurring in short periods of time.

Twice daily, at 12Z and 18Z, the National Weather Service Tropical Prediction Center, located at the National Hurricane Center in Miami, Florida, issues streamline analysis charts for both Pacific and Atlantic Oceans. The streamlines appear as bold, curved lines plotted parallel to surface airflow, with arrows showing wind direction.

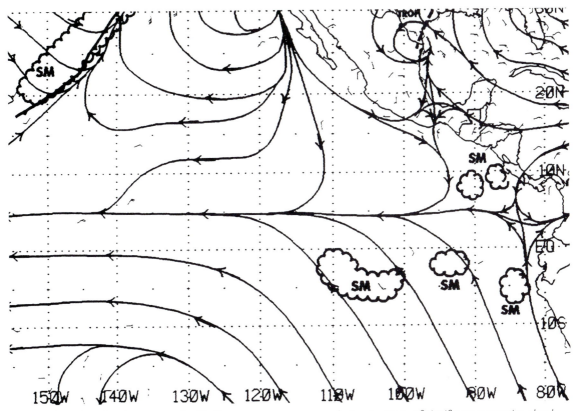

A streamline chart for the eastern Pacific Ocean. Solid lines show wind flow direction, and scalloped areas designate areas of significant convective cloud development.

In addition, these charts show expected movement of surface synoptic (large-scale) features: highs, lows, fronts, troughs, and ridges. Internationally recognized symbols are used to designate tropical systems:

- Circle with a dot inside represents a tropical disturbance
- Circle with an X inside represents a tropical depression
- Circle with center open and spiraling arms represents a tropical storm
- Circle with center filled and spiraling arms represents a hurricane

Two types of wind data are plotted on a streamline chart: actual ship reports and *boundary-layer winds* (winds within 2,000 feet of the Earth's surface). Boundary-layer winds are determined from model forecasts and satellite imagery and are included on charts to indicate wind flow in areas with sparse ship report data.

Regions of significant thunderstorm or rain activity are enclosed with scalloped lines, resembling a hand-drawn cloud, and labeled according to coverage and intensity:

- SCT (scattered showers and rain)
- ISOLD (isolated showers and rain)
- MOD (moderate intensity)
- STG (strong intensity)

Tropical waves and cyclones are noted with their name and latest advisory position. Cyclones are designated using a six-digit code, which provides general information about that feature. For example, the code "150806" placed adjacent to a cyclone would indicate the following: 15 refers to the day of the month when this system became developed and consistent, 08 means it is the eighth tropical storm of that season, and 06 is number of days this system has been under analysis.

During hurricane season in the Northern Hemisphere (June to November) streamline analysis is an important tool in detecting and tracking tropical waves, areas of low pressure that are breeding grounds for development of full-fledged hurricanes.

REGIONAL CHARTS

Regional charts are produced on polar stereographic backgrounds and cover western Atlantic Ocean waters west of 50 degrees west and north of 30 degrees north, including the U.S. East Coast and the central Florida coast. Also covered is the eastern North Pacific Ocean, from the Baja peninsula south to Cabo San Lucas, and north to the Gulf of Alaska, including Prince William Sound as far west as 150 degrees west. Regional products consist of a 24-hour surface forecast and a wind/wave forecast. The Marine Forecast Branch of the Marine Prediction Center (MPC) issues these charts twice daily per ocean for 00Z and 12Z.

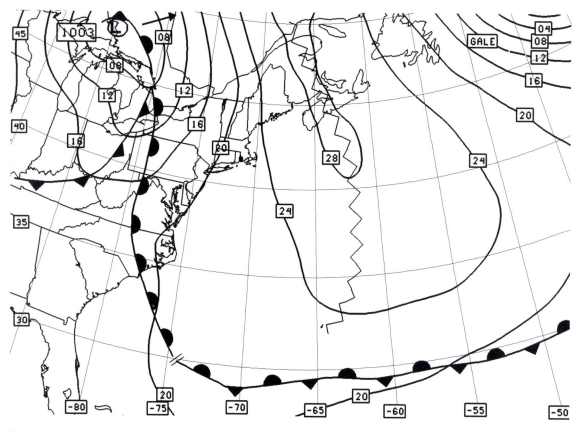

A regional surface forecast chart for the western Atlantic Ocean showing the mid-Atlantic ridge, a stationary front along 30 north, a low-pressure system over the Great Lakes with associated cold and warm fronts, and isobar lines for the entire region in 4-mb intervals.

These are short-range forecast products depicting synoptic and mesoscale features of surface low- and high-pressure systems. Isobars, frontal features, areas of reduced visibility, wind speeds, and significant waves within 1,000 miles of the U.S. East and West Coasts are shown.

Preparation of these charts includes obtaining

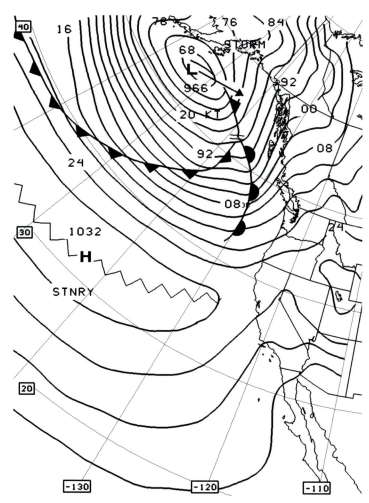

A regional surface forecast chart for the eastern Pacific Ocean showing a developing low-pressure system in the Gulf of Alaska and a high-pressure ridge positioned along 30 north. Note the tight isobar lines surrounding the Alaskan low, indicating strong surface winds. Central pressure is 966 mb, and this system is moving in a southeasterly direction at 20 knots, as annotated on the chart.

wind speeds from Special Sensor Microwave Imagery (SSM/I), received from weather satellites. This data input is especially noteworthy in data-sparse areas where there are no ship or buoy reports. SSM/I aids in short-range prediction of the 24-hour forecast products by enabling comparison of initial data from forecast model output and making necessary adjustments.

Specific features shown on 24-hour surface regional forecast charts are low- and high-pressure center positions with bold three- and four-digit central pressure values underlined or adjacent to the "L" or "H." An arrow displays direction of the system's movement, with speed of motion in knots adjacent to the head of the arrow.

Significant systems have labels depicting whether the system is expected to have gale or storm conditions. If gale or storm conditions are expected in the 24-hour forecast, the appropriate area bears the label "developing gale" or "developing storm." Also displayed are frontal systems (occluded, warm, and cold) and, when appropriate, associated areas of fog, indicating areas of restricted visibility.

Isobars are depicted in increments of 4 mb except for deep systems (e.g., 960 mb), where increments of 8 mb are employed. When 8-mb spacing is used in conjunction with 4-mb spacing, the 1000-mb contour will be dashed to separate 4-mb from 8-mb lines.

ICE CHARTS

Ice is a common feature in high latitudes in both hemispheres, where it affects weather, visibility, and sea

---

✺ *Dry Lines*

Occasionally one sees the notation "dry line" on a weather chart (see pages 105, 110). A *dry line* is a boundary between moist and dry air masses, found frequently in the southwest United States in states such as Texas and Oklahoma. Temperature change across dry lines can be as much as 50°F. Dry air behind a dry line lifts moist air. This can result in thunderstorms and supercell formation, which is conducive to downburst and tornado activity.

Unstable atmospheric conditions produce organized cumulus cloud development, detectable on satellite imagery. Indications of dry line formation are

◆ Sharp transition from clear skies to cumulus

◆ Enhanced cumulus clouds along dry line as compared to adjacent areas

◆ Increased cloud development several hours prior to squall occurrence

---

conditions year round. Locating ice in the North Atlantic begins with an examination of ice charts and broadcasts produced by the International Ice Patrol. These charts and bulletins are available over SSB broadcast frequencies and the INMARSAT-C SafetyNet service.

Text-only ice bulletins are broadcast at 0000Z and 1200Z daily during ice season (February to August), primarily by U.S. Coast Guard Communications Station Boston, Massachusetts (NMF/NIK), and Canadian Coast Guard Radio Station St. John's, Newfoundland (VON).

Ice bulletins are also broadcast by secondary stations, including: METOC Halifax, Nova Scotia (CFH); Canadian Coast Guard Radio Station Halifax (VCS); Radio Station Bracknell, U.K. (GFE); and U.S. Navy Radio Stations Norfolk, Virginia (NAM), and Key West, Florida.

A daily facsimile chart, graphically depicting limits of all known ice, is prepared and broadcast at 1600Z and 1800Z daily. This facsimile chart

```
L9 DE U9

O 311100Z JUL 98
FM COMINTICEPAT GROTON CT
TO COGARD OSC MARTINSBURG WV//CSATGATE//
ADWS OFFUTT AFB NE
AIG EIGHT NINE ONE SIX
USCGC TAHOMA
USNS ZEUS
NWS WASHINGTON DC
BT
UNCLAS //N16170//
STNT41 KNIK 311200
MSGID/CSAT/SAFETYNET/INITIAL//
ADDR/CCODE/1:31:04:01:00/AOW/IIP//
TEXT/BEGIN
SUBJ: INTERNATIONAL ICE PATROL (IIP) BULLETIN
SECURITE
1. 31 JUL 98 1200 UTC INTERNATIONAL ICE PATROL (IIP) BULLETIN.
REPORT POSITION AND TIME OF ALL ICE SIGHTED TO COMINTICEPAT VIA CG
COMMUNICATIONS STATION NMF, NMN, INMARSAT CODE 42, AND ANY CANADIAN
COAST GUARD RADIO STATION.  ALL SHIPS ARE REQUESTED TO MAKE
UNCLASSIFIED SEA SURFACE TEMPERATURE AND WEATHER REPORTS TO
COMINTICEPAT EVERY SIX HOURS WHEN WITHIN THE LATITUDES OF 40N AND
52N AND LONGITUDES 39W AND 57W.  IT IS NOT NECESSARY TO MAKE THESE
REPORTS IF A ROUTINE WEATHER REPORT IS MADE TO METEO WASHINGTON DC.
ALL MARINERS ARE URGED TO USE EXTREME CAUTION WHEN TRANSITING
NEAR THE GRAND BANKS SINCE ICE MAY BE IN THE AREA.  THIS BULLETIN
IS ALSO LOCATED ON OUR WWW SITE AT THE FOLLOWING ADDRESS:
WWW.RDC.USCG.MIL/IIPPAGES/IIPPRODS.HTML
2. ESTIMATED LIMIT OF ALL KNOWN ICE:    FROM THE NEWFOUNDLAND COAST
NEAR 4748N 5247W TO 4745N 5130W TO 5000N 4815W TO 5200N 4830W TO
5600N 5300W THEN NORTHWARD. THE ICEBERG LIMIT NORTH OF 52N IS
OBTAINED FROM CANADIAN ICE SERVICE, OTTAWA CANADA.
3. THE FOLLOWING RADAR TARGETS ARE OUTSIDE THE LIMIT OF ALL KNOWN
ICE:  4455N 4448W, 4638N 4501W, 4647N 4534W.
4. THERE ARE SCATTERED ICEBERGS AND GROWLERS NORTH OF 5100N AND WEST
OF 5100W WITHIN THE LIMIT OF ALL KNOWN ICE.
5.   THIS IS THE FINAL ICE BULLETIN FOR THE 1998 SEASON.
INTERNATIONAL ICE PATROL THANKS YOU FOR YOUR COOPERATION IN
REPORTING ICE SIGHTINGS, SEA SURFACE TEMPERATURE, AND WEATHER
INFORMATION DURING THE 1998 SEASON.  WE REQUEST THAT YOU CONTINUE
TO ADDRESS ICE SIGHTINGS SOUTH OF 52N TO COMINTICEPAT GROTON CT.
PLEASE ADDRESS OTHER ICE SIGHTINGS AND REQUESTS FOR ICE
INFORMATION TO ENVIRONMENT CANADA ICE CENTRE OTTAWA OR NIMA
NAVSAFETY BETHESDA MD.
END//
BT
```

International Ice Patrol text bulletin describing ice conditions on 31 July 1998. This bulletin is sent out via Navtex and Inmarsat satellite systems and posted on the Internet.

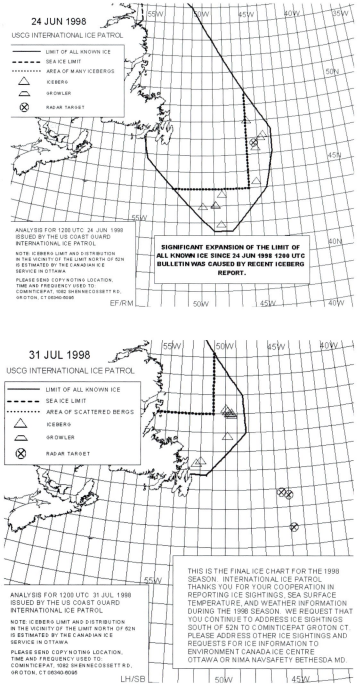

Ice charts for June and July, showing limit of all known ice (LAKI). Note the significant reduction in ice from June to July caused by warming conditions in northern latitudes.

is also placed on COMSAT's Inmarsat-A Faxmail server.

Ice concentration is greatest in April, with the southernmost ice limit occurring in May. Records show the median ice limit at the Tail of the Grand Bank (42 to 20 degrees north), but ice has extended as far south as 38 to 30 degrees north (1990). The eastern limit of ice is near Flemish Cap, a bank near 47 north/45 west.

An interesting aspect of iceberg tracking is that approximately half of the icebergs found near the limit of all known ice (LAKI) were previously undetected. For this to occur, icebergs had to have slipped by the various detection means (ships, aircraft, satellite imagery) or have been created in the LAKI region. One explanation of this phenomenon is that icebergs split into two or more pieces as they approach warm water near the southern extent of LAKI, and this splitting is most likely a part of the melting process.

July and August are months when icebergs are at a minimum. Statistics from the International Ice Patrol for past ice seasons track the amount of ice traveling south. In April 1995, for example, there were 334 icebergs spotted south of 48 degrees north; in May 405 bergs crossed the 48 north parallel heading south; June had 218 bergs south of 48 north; and in July there were 39 bergs spotted south of 48 north. There were no significant sightings in August, and, in general, most ice was found north of 41 north, between 45 and 55 west longitude.

Detailed information on ice charts can be obtained from the International Ice Patrol (see appendix 3).

WAVE AND SEA STATE CHARTS

Waves fall into three categories: ripples, seas, and swells. Waves begin as ripples and grow, with increasing wind strength, to seas and then mature into swells. There are three ingredients to wave formation and growth:

- **Wind strength**, measured using the Beaufort wind scale
- **Duration** (the time, in hours, that a given wind blows over an area of ocean)
- **Fetch** (the distance, in nautical miles, over which a given wind blows)

Maximum wave height is linked to a combination of wind strength, duration, and fetch. Large waves are found where there are strong winds blowing over open ocean for extended periods, such as in the Southern Ocean.

Waves are not symmetrical in shape. Crests are by nature steeper and narrower than troughs, with sea level slightly below half a wave's height. Waves develop slowly: on average it takes many hours of sustained wind at any given speed before maximum wave height is reached. A Beaufort Force 3 breeze (7–10 knots) needs eight hours to develop a 2-foot sea, the maximum height it will produce with unlimited fetch. A Beaufort Force 8 wind (34–40 knots) requires 40 hours to develop its maximum wave height with unlimited fetch, 28 feet.

In deep water—where depth is greater than half a wavelength—there is a general relationship between length, period, and speed for fully developed and mature waves:

$$L \text{ (in feet)} = 5 \times P \text{ (in seconds) squared}$$

$$S \text{ (speed)} = 3 \times P \text{ (in seconds)}$$

A sea state analysis is produced each day for the Atlantic and Pacific Oceans, as well as two 48-hour sea state forecasts. The analyses are prepared using ship reports and are overlaid and compared with surface analysis charts.

SEA STATE ANALYSIS

A sea state analysis is issued once a day per ocean (12Z in the Atlantic Ocean and 00Z in the Pacific Ocean) at the times when the largest number of ship observations are available. Primary swell direction is depicted using large black arrows. Where appropriate, maximum and minimum combined wave height values (approximately one-third the height of the wind wave added to the height of the swell wave) are shown with the abbreviation of "MAX" or "MIN" adjacent to the maximum or minimum values.

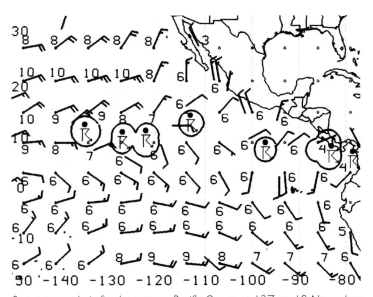

Sea state analysis for the eastern Pacific Ocean at 12Z on 19 November 1998. Wind speed is given in knots and sea height in feet. Also note that areas of significant convective activity, such as thunderstorms, are annotated, in this case with a circle and thunderstorm symbol.

Primary swell direction arrows are based on actual ship observation reports, and during winter months ice edges are displayed as a bold jagged line. Sea state analyses highlight where the most significant combined sea and swell wave heights prevail and, when combined with surface analyses, provide a complete picture of surface weather conditions. Wave forecasts are overlaid on corresponding weather analysis charts to ensure that systems such as lows, highs, and fronts relate correctly to sea state. Sea height contour lines—called *isopleths*—are drawn either in feet or meters, with maximum sea height noted for specific areas. Height is indicated in feet is used on charts covering U.S. coastal and offshore areas, and in meters for international coverage.

48-HOUR SEA STATE FORECASTS

Forty-eight-hour sea state forecasts are generated twice daily, for 00Z and 12Z, and are based on significant wave forecast computer models and observations. Combined sea heights are depicted using 1-meter contours with maximum or minimum combined sea state values underlined and labeled with the abbreviation "MAX" or "MIN." Sea state forecasts use large black arrows to show predominant swell direction, which is actually a vector resolution of all sea and swell activity in a

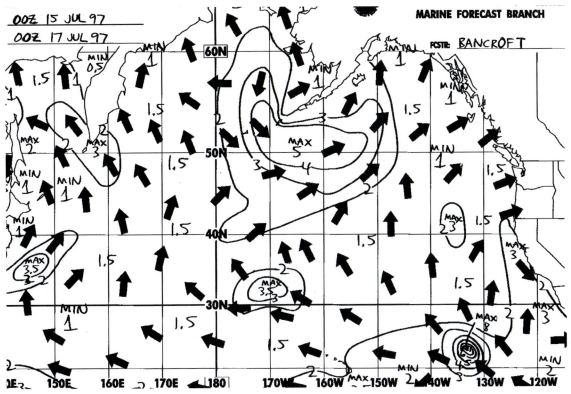

A 48-hour sea state forecast for the Pacific Ocean showing moderate sea conditions, with the exception of 8-meter seas noted at the bottom right corner of the chart, and 5-meter seas near Kodiak Island in the Gulf of Alaska. There is also a small pocket of 3.5-meter seas in the mid-Pacific associated with a local disturbance. Those 8-meter seas to the southeast are associated with a tropical low-pressure system, which would be detailed on a surface analysis chart for the same synoptic time.

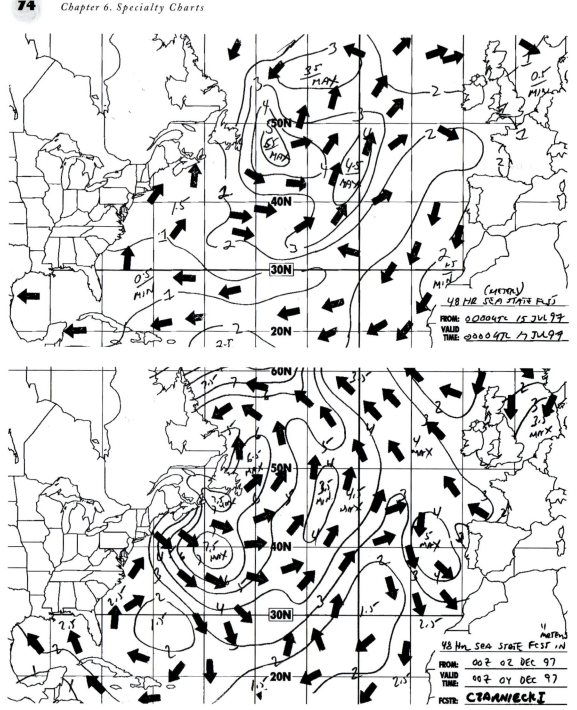

Two 48-hour sea state forecasts for the Atlantic Ocean, showing conditions in July and December. Valid time, seen at the bottom right corner, indicates the date and time when features shown on the chart are predicted to exist.

"From" time denotes when data used to prepare the chart were gathered. Black arrows show the direction of combined seas and swells but do not indicate wave speed or height. Wave height is marked separately in meters.

given area. Arrows only represent direction; they are equal in size and do not reflect wave height or period.

Chart accuracy depends on the number and accuracy of real-time observations, so actual ship reports are critical to producing these charts. In the Atlantic Ocean the 1200Z (0700 East Coast time) analysis coincides with the highest number of accurate ship reports, since these readings are taken during daylight and when crews are most alert. In the Pacific the 0000Z (1600 Pacific Coast Time) analysis is scheduled for similar reasons.

Similar to sea state analyses, a 48-hour sea state forecast will provide a complete picture of surface conditions when used in conjunction with

the 48-hour surface forecast and will highlight where significant combined sea and swell wave heights will prevail.

24-HOUR WIND/WAVE FORECASTS

This chart depicts 24-hour forecasts of wind in increments of 5 knots and significant wave heights (isopleths of combined sea and swell in 3-foot increments). In winter the potential for superstructure icing—sea conditions that will bring water on board and thereby cause ice buildup—is indicated by a half moon crossed by one or two lines depending on whether light or heavy accumulation is expected.

Along the Atlantic coast large seas can build

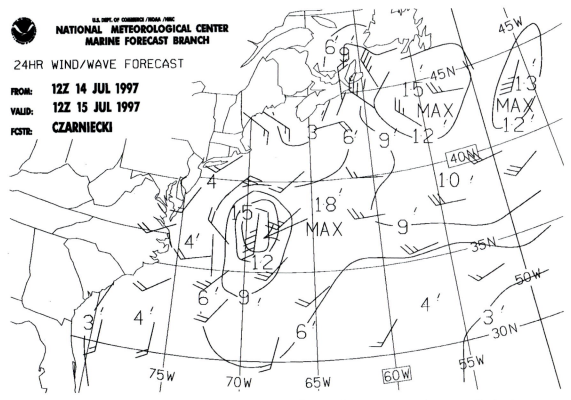

This 24-hour wind/wave chart for the western Atlantic shows sea height in feet, representing changes in sea height using solid contour lines (isopleths). Notice the 18-foot maximum seas near the center of a low-pressure system, its presence inferred by the counterclockwise-flowing wind arrows.

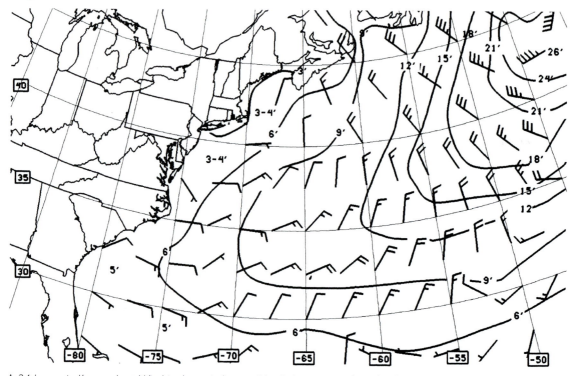

A 24-hour wind/wave chart. Wind is shown in knots with wind arrows, and sea height in feet with contour lines drawn at 3-foot intervals.

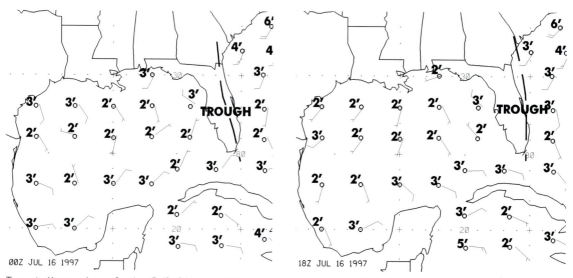

Two wind/wave charts for the Gulf of Mexico, 18 hours apart, with sea height in feet and wind arrows. Note the trough of low pressure over Florida. This weather feature is displayed because localized disturbances under this trough may briefly produce sea heights greater than shown in its vicinity.

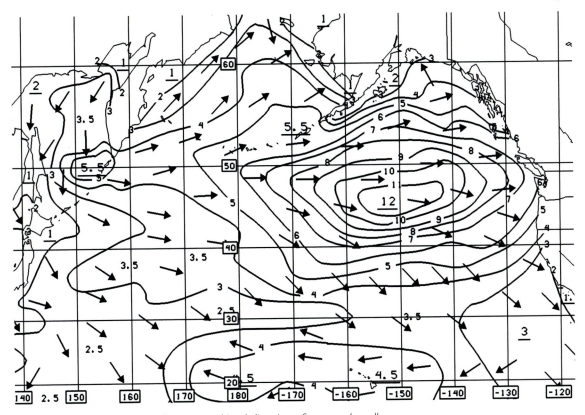

A 48-hour sea state forecast showing combined direction of seas and swells using large arrows and sea height in meters.

near the Gulf Stream when strong north and northeast winds blow against the northward moving current. Seas often develop exaggerated height and short periods, and frequently evolve into breaking seas. Breaking seas are dangerous to small vessels since wave energy is directed horizontally, having the potential to damage or capsize an otherwise seaworthy vessel.

To warn of abnormal Gulf Stream wave conditions the NWS issues a north wall bulletin. As mentioned earlier, the term "north wall" refers to the northern edge (wall) of the Gulf Stream where the stream's speed tends to be the strongest, producing the highest and shortest seas.

North wall areas are shown on wind/wave forecasts using cross-hatching and labeled "Gulf Stream north wall." Seas and winds within a hatched area are likely to be twice the height and speed found outside a north wall region.

A useful technique in using wind/wave charts is to overlay them with corresponding surface analysis charts and forecasts. Surface charts and wind/wave charts are produced purposely with the same scale and format so mariners can place these charts over each other and easily analyze and compare wind and sea state conditions.

OCEANOGRAPHIC PRODUCTS

Sea surface temperature (SST) analyses are prepared twice weekly by the National Weather Service for Atlantic and Pacific waters. In the Pacific a northern chart includes the nearshore

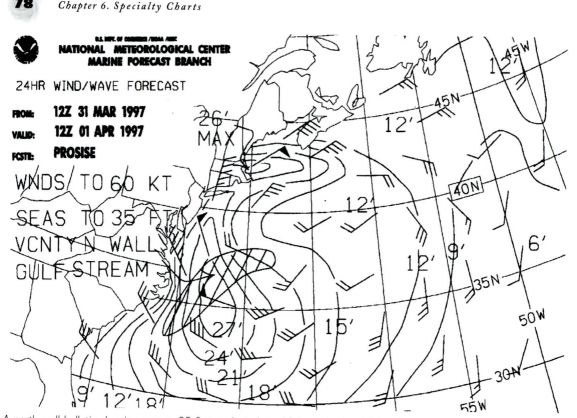

A north wall bulletin showing seas to 35 feet and winds to 60 knots in the vicinity of the Gulf Stream's north edge, or wall, as annotated with hatched lines.

waters of Washington and Oregon and the coastal waters of Vancouver Island and Queen Charlotte Sound in Canada. Geographical limits of this chart are from 53 north to 40 north and west to the 136 west meridian.

A southern chart includes all of California, the Baja peninsula, and the coastal waters of western Mexico, south to Puerto Vallarta. This chart includes the area from 41 to 20 north latitude and west to 136 west longitude.

Atlantic charts cover the Gulf of Maine, south of New England, and the Southeast coast. All charts incorporate a variety of in-situ observations including ships, fixed buoy reports, drifting buoys, XBTs (expendable bathy-thermographs), coastal observations, MAREPS (mariner reports), MCSST (multi-channel sea surface temperatures) derived from NOAA's polar orbiting satellites, and, most importantly, Advanced Very High Resolution Radiometer (AVHRR) satellite imagery.

Sea surface temperature gradient information, as well as prominent oceanographic features (upwelling boundaries and eddies), is identified and combined with in-situ reports. Lastly, isotherms from previous analysis are used as a reference.

7

Satellite Images

Satellite imagery provides useful and significant information on past, present, and future weather. Each cloud swirl, streak, and puff can be associated with a particular weather system or phenomenon. And when images are viewed with a good understanding of weather dynamics, analyses and forecasts can be made with confidence.

SATELLITES

There are two types of weather satellites: high-altitude geostationary, and low-altitude polar orbiting. Receiving imagery from geostationary satellites requires a tracking dish, while imagery from polar orbiting satellites is received using a passive helix antenna that does not need to be locked onto a satellite.

Satellites provide both visible-spectrum (VIS) and infrared (IR) imagery of the Earth. VIS and IR images are received simultaneously and resemble black-and-white photographs.

On VIS images, shades of black and white—there are 256 shades of gray that make up a black-and-white image—represent the amount of light reflected back into space. Large thunderstorms, being dense, reflect back 92 percent of the light hitting them, so they appear bright white on an image. Water surfaces, such as oceans, lakes, and rivers, reflect back only 9 percent of the light hitting them, so they appear dark gray or black.

IR imagery, on the other hand, shows energy being radiated from landmasses, water surfaces, and cloud tops. This radiated energy is represented as temperature and is displayed using 256 distinct shades of gray, as with VIS imagery. High clouds, which are very cold, appear bright white in IR images, and land, which is comparatively warm, appears dark. Although 256 shades of gray are available for imaging, the human eye can only detect 15 to 20 shades of gray, so bands of reflectivity are used for displaying VIS images and bands of temperature for IR.

Used together during daylight hours, VIS and

IR images provide information on cloud location, thickness, height, and movement. At night only IR images are available. (Satellite imagery is available continuously from geostationary satellites; images are available from polar orbiting satellites only when the satellite is passing over an observer, which occurs approximately every two to four hours, depending on the observer's latitude.)

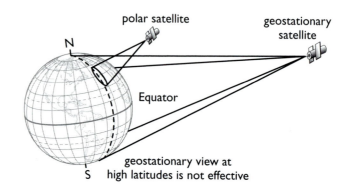

Satellite imagery can also provide an indirect indication of sea state: when water surfaces are calm and skies are clear, the sun's rays will often reflect off the water, causing a bright spot called *sun glint*.

Polar orbiting satellites circle the Earth from pole to pole at an altitude of about 500 miles, passing over a fixed point approximately every two to four hours depending on latitude. Geostationary satellites orbit at an altitude of some 23,000 miles, providing continuous coverage of the same area of the Earth's surface. Geostationary satellites are not effective for viewing the higher latitudes (approaching the poles) due to the increasing angle between the satellite's sensors and the Earth's surface. Both can provide VIS and IR imagery.

CLOUDS

The most important weather information supplied by satellite imagery is cloud data. Analysis of cloud altitude, shape, temperature, and movement goes a long way toward explaining what the associated air mass is doing.

There are basically two types of clouds: flat and puffy. Flat clouds are known scientifically as *stratus* and puffy clouds as *cumulus*.

Flat clouds, showing an absence of vertical development, reflect a stable atmosphere with minimal vertical mixing or convective activity.

Ephemeris Data

Ephemeris data, also called *e-data* or *orbital elements*, describe the paths satellites follow around the Earth. When satellite weather images are captured, e-data are combined with precise information on time and receiver position to permit the placement of latitude and longitude lines and geopolitical boundaries. Continuous time and position information is normally obtained by connecting a satellite system to a Global Positioning System (GPS) receiver. E-data, however, must be inputted manually and fortunately only need to be updated every few weeks. Obtaining and entering e-data is straightforward: files are downloaded from the Internet and read by the system's software to update satellite paths. The manufacturers of satellite weather systems provide their own methods for obtaining e-data. Another source of e-data for U.S. NOAA satellites is the Ocean and Environmental Sensing (OCENS) homepage on the Internet (see appendix 3). E-data are downloaded to your computer as an ELEMENTS.DAT file, which is automatically read by a system's software. Additional Internet sites provide e-data for these and other satellites such as the MIR space station and the U.S. space shuttle.

Puffy clouds, on the other hand, indicate vertical mixing, with warm air rising and cold air sinking. This mixing causes both cloud formation and wind, the strength of which depends on the local temperature gradient between warm and cold air. An extreme example of a puffy cloud is a thunderhead, which bears a special name, *cumulonimbus*—cumulo for puffy and nimbus for rain. Cumulonimbus clouds develop through all levels of the atmosphere and upon reaching the jet stream are blown downwind, producing the characteristic anvil head.

Both flat and puffy clouds are further divided into three altitude categories. Low clouds, called *stratus*, are found below 8,000 feet (2,424 m); middle clouds, called *alto*, are between 8,000 and 18,000 feet; and high clouds, or *cirrus*, are composed of ice crystals and found above 18,000 feet (5,454 meters). The average cloud-top temperature for low clouds is 42°F; for middle clouds, 10°F; and for high clouds, 30°F. Cloud temperature is shown in infrared satellite imagery and reflects vertical cloud development, which in turn indicates the strength of surface weather conditions.

Cloud shapes (flat or puffy) are combined with the three altitude levels (low, middle, and high) in cloud designations. A high, flat cloud is called a *cirrostratus*, and a midlevel flat cloud is an *altostratus*. A low, flat cloud is simply a *stratus*. A high puffy cloud is a *cirrocumulus*, a midlevel puffy cloud is an *altocumulus*, and a low-level puffy cloud is a *stratocumulus*. The ten basic cloud classifications are listed here, from high to low.

◆ **Cirrus (Ci).** These are high, detached clouds composed of ice crystals, having a fibrous or wispy appearance, without texture, and white in color. Tufted cirrus clouds are known as "mare's tails." They appear bright white on infrared (IR) images as these clouds are very cold, but they may not be readily apparent on visible-spectrum (VIS) imagery since they are usually thin and reflect little light.

◆ **Cirrocumulus (Cc).** This layer of small white flakes or cotton balls, without shadows and arranged in lines, is a good indicator of upper-level wind direction and speed. When jet stream winds exceed 70–100 knots, these clouds align themselves perpendicular to the turbulent wind flow. At lesser wind speeds the clouds move in lines, or *streets*, parallel to wind flow. This dynamic is actually true of any cirrus-level cloud but is most visible in the case of cirrocumulus.

◆ **Cirrostratus (Cs).** This high cloud is a transparent white sheet composed of ice crystals and covering the sky. Seen as cold clouds on IR imagery, cirrostratus are often apparent in visible imagery too, depending on density and ability to reflect light.

◆ **Altocumulus (Ac).** Like so many cotton balls, connected or disconnected, altocumulus clouds are often elongated, covering much of the sky. These midlevel clouds are good reflectors of light, but appear in IR images more as a light shade of gray than a bright white.

◆ **Altostratus (As).** This is a sheet of clouds, midlevel and flat, gray or bluish in color.

◆ **Stratocumulus (Sc).** These low-level, puffy clouds exist in patches and rolls, appearing gray with darker patches.

◆ **Stratus (St).** A uniform, low-level cloud layer resembling fog, but not resting on the surface, stratus clouds are gray in color on IR images since they are low and warm, and often bright white on VIS imagery as they reflect light well when dense.

◆ **Nimbostratus (Ns).** A low or midlevel rainy cloud, nimbostratus appear dark gray on both visible and IR satellite images.

◆ **Cumulus (Cu).** These are thick, puffy clouds with vertical development, billowy upper surfaces, and flat bases. They appear bright white on VIS images due to density and gray on IR because they are low and warm.

◆ **Cumulonimbus (Cb).** Large clouds with pronounced vertical development, cumulonimbus have a fibrous texture in their upper parts and often spread out in the shape of an anvil. They are bright white on both VIS and IR imagery due to cold tops and dense structure.

Though clouds might at first glance appear to lack easily discerned patterns, there are distinct and recognizable cloud patterns associated with the formation, growth, and dissipation of lows, highs, troughs, and ridges. A cumulonimbus cloud represents mixing throughout the atmosphere, likely bringing rain and gusty winds. Stratus clouds represent a stable low-level atmosphere, with little wind. Of all the cloud types, cirrus and cirrostratus are especially to be watched, as these are the first harbingers of an advancing warm front or occlusion associated with low-pressure systems. Cumuli are fair-weather clouds forming over the land during daytime heating. Towering cumulus clouds indicate substantial convection; expect showers and squalls. Any clouds of the Cu type observed over land at dawn are more likely to be stratocumulus than true cumulus. At sea, unlike over land, large active cumuli may be found by night as well as by day, there being no appreciable diurnal temperature variations at the sea surface.

Clear areas are normally associated with high-pressure regions, where air masses are of low humidity and therefore relatively cloud free. Low-pressure areas, on the other hand, have varying degrees of cloud development depending on the amount of moisture present and the extent of convective (vertical) and advective (horizontal) motion within the atmosphere.

THE JET STREAM

To understand cloud patterns, a basic knowledge of jet stream behavior is necessary (see chapters 1 and 5), since it is the undulating waves of jet stream winds that bring together (converge) and separate (diverge) air masses at the surface and result in weather systems and their associated cloud patterns. Just to review, jet stream winds are

plotted on upper-air charts showing their north–south undulations, called ridges and troughs, which reflect the movement of large masses of cold and warm air. As previously noted, in the Northern Hemisphere the jet stream follows a clockwise motion in ridges and a counterclockwise motion in troughs; the opposite is true in the Southern Hemisphere.

The jet stream can be located by noting where well-defined bands of cirrus clouds lie on satellite imagery: cirrus clouds often define the jet stream's northernmost edge. It is on this edge that warm, moist air from the south meets cool, dry air from the north, producing upper-level condensation—cirrus clouds. When high moisture levels exist in the upper atmosphere (troposphere), cirrus clouds form easily, making jet stream location straightforward. Both IR and VIS imagery are used to locate cirrus and cirrostratus clouds associated with the jet stream. While cirrus clouds appear wispy and linear, cirrostratus appear thick and lumpy and are very stable, high clouds associated with well-developed weather systems. Cirrus-level clouds generally flow parallel to jet stream motion, but if jet stream speed exceeds 70–100 knots turbulent flow will often cause transverse cloud bands (clouds perpendicular to jet stream flow) to form. When looking for well-defined jet stream flow on satellite images, remember the following:

- Look for shadows on lower clouds produced by high-level cirrus.
- Locate large cirrus cloud shields (large masses of clouds of roughly equal length and width).
- Locate long cirrus cloud bands.
- Look for billow clouds.
- Locate transverse cloud bands; when associated with intense or developing weather, these should be watched carefully.

In some cases locating cirrus clouds can be complicated. Although IR shows cold cirrus clouds as bright white, if cirrus are thin the IR sensor may be contaminated by backscatter from warmer low-level clouds (more gray in color) and not reveal the true extent of cirrus clouds. VIS shows reflected light and will reveal well-formed cirrus as white streaks, but if cirrus are not well connected visible light may not reflect well and the cloud will appear more gray than white. Referring to 500-mb charts is very useful when looking at satellite images and will quickly reveal where the strongest flow is located. These charts are found on the Internet (see appendix 3 for addresses).

TROUGHS AND RIDGES

Distinctive cloud shapes form in the vicinity of the jet stream depending on the extent of both horizontal and vertical mixing of warm, moist air and cold, dry air. The amplitude and length of ridges and troughs directly influence cloud shape and also indicate surface weather feature development. High-amplitude troughs tend to pull large amounts of cold, dry air south into regions of warm, moist air, bringing cloudiness and precipitation to the region where the two air masses meet, generally on the east side of a trough.

Troughs can often be located by noting a shift in upper-level wind flow (as seen by cloud pattern) and by recognizing that clear air usually exists to the west of a trough (cold and low humidity) and clouds to the east (cold air cooling warm air to its dew point).

Ridges are often found using IR images.

Cirrus clouds tend to form at the point where a ridge turns, and although cirrus clouds are sometimes difficult to see on VIS images (they are thin and do not reflect light well), they appear bright white (high and cold) on IR imagery.

LOWS AND HIGHS

The location of low-pressure systems is of prime interest since these systems usually bring the strongest winds and largest seas. With practice the central pressure of a low and the speed and direction of its winds can be estimated by observing upper- and low-level clouds on satellite images.

Low-pressure systems fall into three general categories: thermal lows (sea breezes), air mass lows (midlatitude systems), and tropical lows (depressions, storms, and hurricanes). Each has a distinctive cloud pattern and classic stages of development. Midlatitude lows, for example, normally form on the surface under or to the east of an upper-level trough. A cloud shape called a *baroclinic leaf* is the first cloud to appear as a surface low forms. A *vorticity cloud* and a *deformation cloud* follow in succession. After these three cloud regions form and then come together, the system takes on a comma shape, the signature of a well-developed low-pressure system.

Surface high-pressure regions, which are

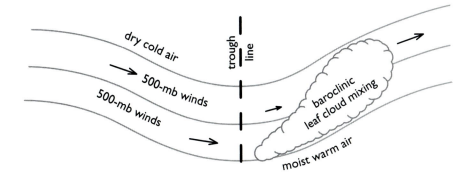

A baroclinic leaf cloud provides the first indication of a developing low on the east side of an upper-level trough. The cloud forms as warm and cold air masses mix.

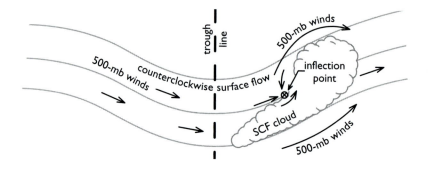

A vorticity cloud appears when a baroclinic leaf cloud develops an inflection point and then counterclockwise flow and a low-pressure center exists on the surface.

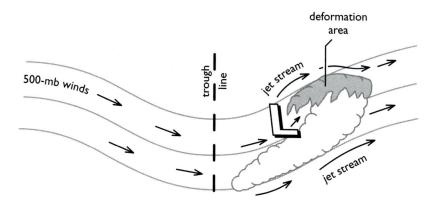

After a vorticity cloud forms and the low begins to develop, the top of the cloud is "deformed" to the north by jet stream flow moving around the system. This is because jet stream flow from the south is now perpendicular to the flow on the north side.

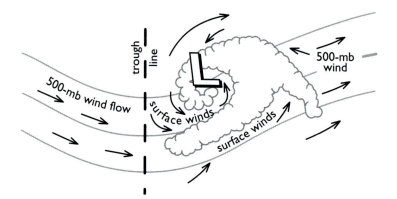

Now the system is a fully developed low with the signature "comma" shape, positioned under the upper-level trough.

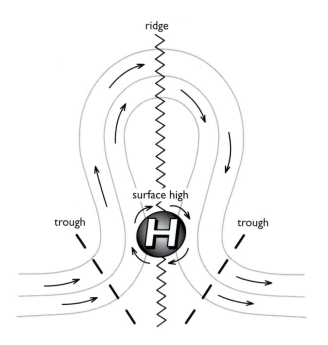

A well-developed surface- and upper-level high is called a blocking or omega high—its shape resembles the Greek letter omega (Ω). Approaching surface lows are forced north or stalled in troughs to the east and west of the high. Omega blocks often remain in place for days or weeks.

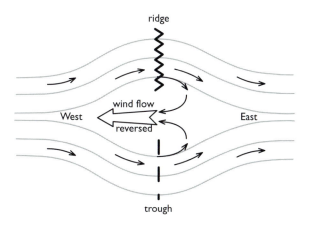

A reverse block in the jet stream causes stream winds to blow from east to west, against the normal flow. This occurs when an upper-level ridge is situated directly north of an upper-level trough.

most often cloud-free, can be located in satellite imagery since their outer edges are often rimmed with clouds. Clouds around a high will indicate the extent of troughing to the west and east and, by the shape of the cloud line, the width and amplitude of that troughing.

A well-developed surface- and upper-level high, with a central pressure of 1030 mb or more, is called a *blocking* or *omega high* (see chapter 5) and will cause an approaching low-pressure system either to stall or to go north around the surface high.

A special type of high pressure feature is a *reverse block*, in which an upper-atmosphere high-pressure area is situated directly north of an upper-atmosphere low, resulting in jet stream winds blowing from east to west between the two systems. This phenomenon pushes the advance of weather systems to the south of their normal track, often bringing unseasonable cold weather to midlatitudes. Satellite imagery will show these features by the location and shape of cloud shields, bands, and lines.

COMPARISON OF IMAGERY AND CHARTS

By comparing weather charts and satellite imagery, as we will in chapter 8, the development and movement of weather features such as lows and highs and their associated cold and warm fronts can be closely monitored. In particular, when satellite images are examined in conjunction with 500-mb upper-air charts,

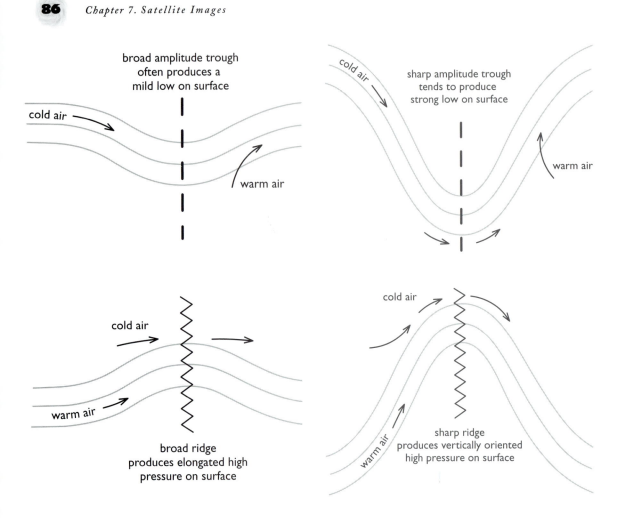

Various shapes of troughs and ridges in the upper atmosphere.

areas of likely low formation can first be identified on the 500-mb chart and then matched with cloud patterns on satellite imagery. This technique reveals the type and extent of low development. The opposite approach can also be taken if a distinctive low-pressure formation is seen on satellite imagery for which no corresponding trough is seen on a 500-mb chart. In this second scenario, rapid changes are taking place within the atmosphere and the original 500-mb forecast will likely be revised to reflect actual conditions. Thus the juxtaposition of satellite images with surface and upper-air weather charts allows the comparison of analyses and forecasts derived from computer models with real-time events.

For example, RILs—intense, rapidly developing low-pressure systems, often referred to as "meteorological bombs" due to their tight and symmetrical isobar lines—develop in 12 to 24 hours (see chapters 1 and 5). Weather charts, prepared and broadcast every six hours, often do not provide much warning of these events, but satellite imagery will show the clouds associated with these systems thickening, lowering, and forming into the tight "comma cloud" associated with low-pressure systems.

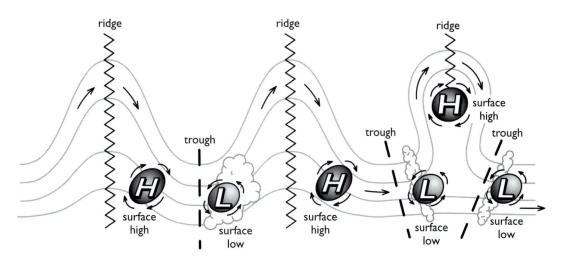

Alternating troughs and ridges in the jet stream with associated surface highs and lows.

Of course, a perceptive observer on the scene will detect cloud formation associated with an intense low and have some warning of its approach. The low-technology clues of a developing storm must not be forgotten—a falling barometer, increasing wind speed, changing wind direction, and building seas and swells.

8

Integrating Satellite Images with Weather Charts

This chapter juxtaposes satellite images with corresponding surface and upper-air weather charts, providing a more complete view of weather systems. Though most of these images are for East Coast and Atlantic events, flow patterns and concepts are applicable to all areas of the world.

It is important in weather analysis and forecasting to understand how low- and high-pressure systems are related to upper-air troughs and ridges, and the dynamics of how these systems form, develop, and dissipate.

Understanding weather is largely pattern recognition. If the sequences of events shown in these examples are studied, understood, and internalized, they can be used as benchmarks for gauging and evaluating future weather.

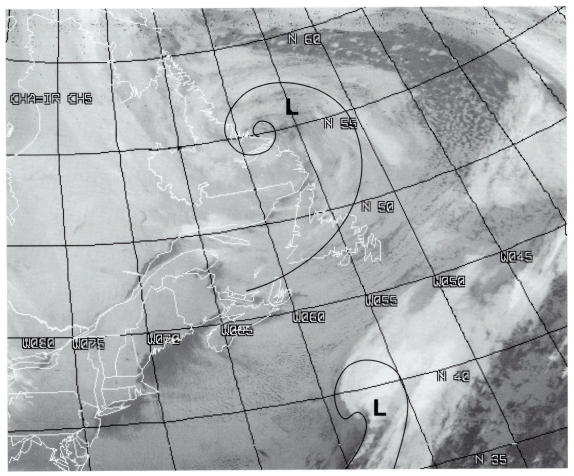

1 January 1997

A well-defined and closed upper-level trough over Newfoundland (55N/55W) on 1 January 1997 gave support to a surface low-pressure system (upper L) that quickly developed into a storm. A distinctive comma cloud shape (highlighted) can be seen on this infrared (IR) satellite image defining the low's counterclockwise circulation. Notice the areas of dry, cold air (no clouds to the west of the low's center) and the mixing of moist maritime air with cold upper air (cloudy area to the east of the low's center).

A second low (lower L), developing into a storm, is found on the image at 38 north/58 west, confirmed by the hooked comma cloud and dense clouds found in that region. Note also the cloud-free area just off the Maine coast where dry and cold continental air has not yet mixed sufficiently with moist maritime air to form the clouds seen farther offshore.

Wind direction can be determined by noting cloud alignment. Cloud streets generally orient themselves parallel to wind flow, and puffy cumulus-type clouds represent areas of turbulence, where cold and warm air are mixing.

Two low-pressure systems are shown on this IR image and 48-hour surface forecast chart. Compare the latitude and longitude coordinates for the lows on the image and the chart. Note how the more northerly of the two lows shows the beginning of a counterclockwise comma-cloud shape, while the southerly low is still in the baroclinic leaf stage. Low-level warm clouds appear gray and are scattered around the edge of high pressure.

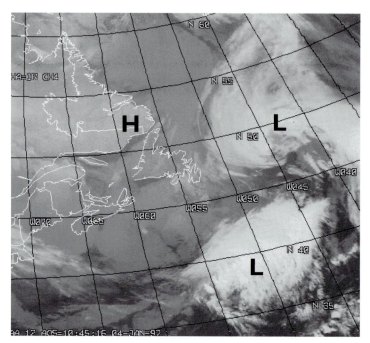

4 January 1997

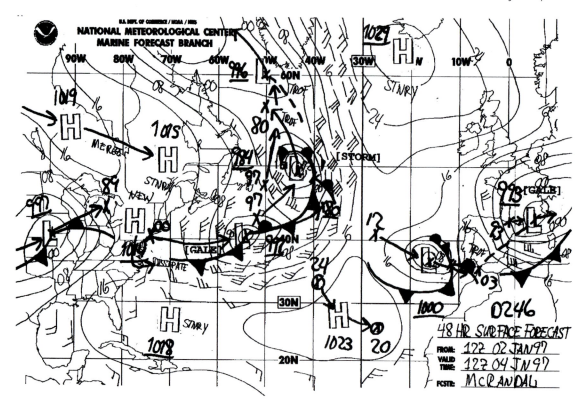

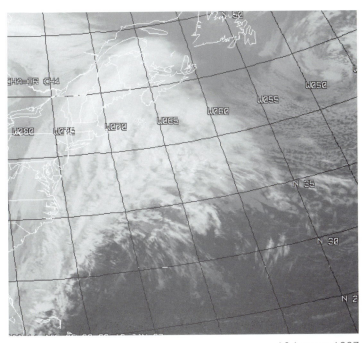

The beginnings of two low-pressure systems are shown on an IR image taken on 10 January; a 96-hour surface forecast chart valid on 12 January shows the fully developed systems. A baroclinic leaf cloud is seen on the left side of the IR image. Bright white clouds indicate cold cloud top temperature. Note the cloud-free high-pressure area to the southeast. Cloud streets show surface wind flow. Observe the direction of low movement as shown on the 96-hour forecast.

10 January 1997

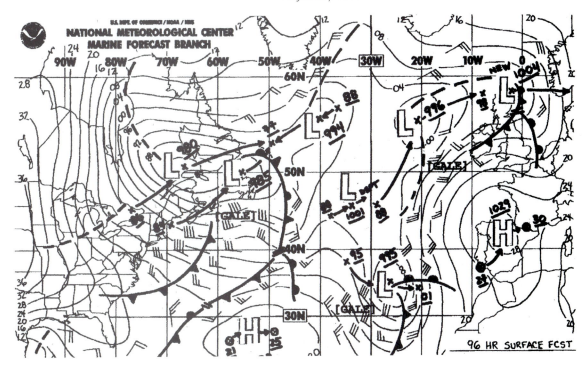

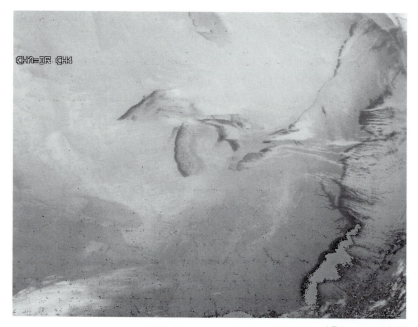

17 January 1997

A large high-pressure system is shown in this IR image and surface analysis chart for 17 January 1997. Note the clear skies over the eastern United States, with increasing clouds over the Atlantic Ocean in the vicinity of the Gulf Stream. Here cold continental air is mixing with warm, moist Gulf Stream air to produce abundant clouds. Clouds appear over the western Great Lakes where a trough line is shown on the surface chart. Compare wind flow on the chart with the cloud lines on the image.

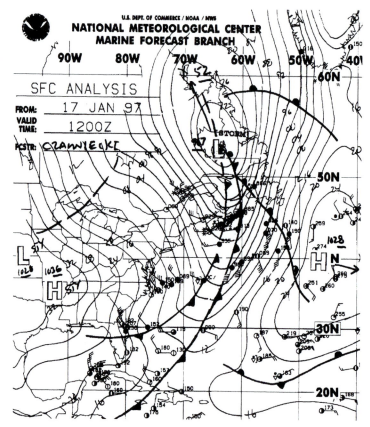

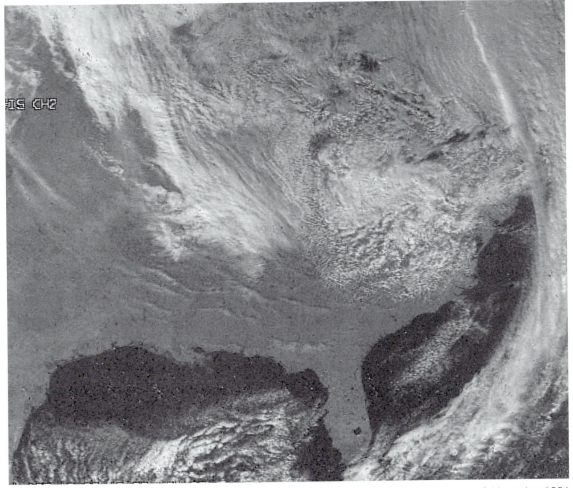

9 November 1996

A crisp visible spectrum (VIS) image of the southeastern United States showing a cold front passing off the East Coast. Visible images show reflected light with bright white, indicating dense and highly reflective surfaces such as clouds; nonreflective surfaces, such as land and the surface of lakes and oceans, appear darker.

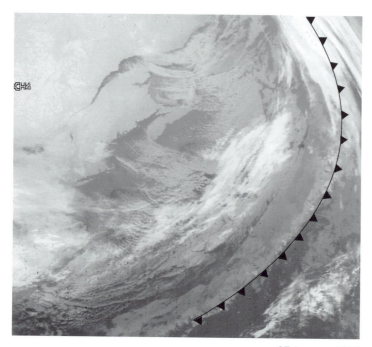

27 January 1997

Two IR images and two surface analysis charts show a succession of lows in January 1997. On 27 January a storm near Greenland has a trailing cold front (highlighted on the 27 January IR image) reaching down to the middle Atlantic; note how Nova Scotia and the Canadian Maritimes are under clear skies. On 28 January a new set of fronts has appeared over the East Coast. Note the clear skies associated with offshore high pressure. Low-level clouds near high pressure are gray, indicating warm cloud top temperatures.

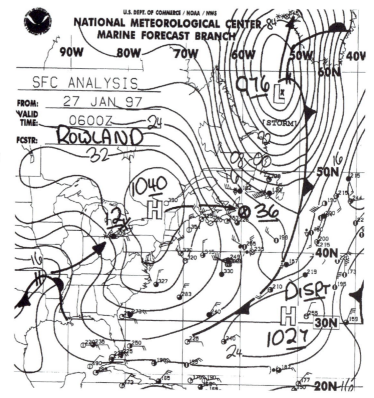

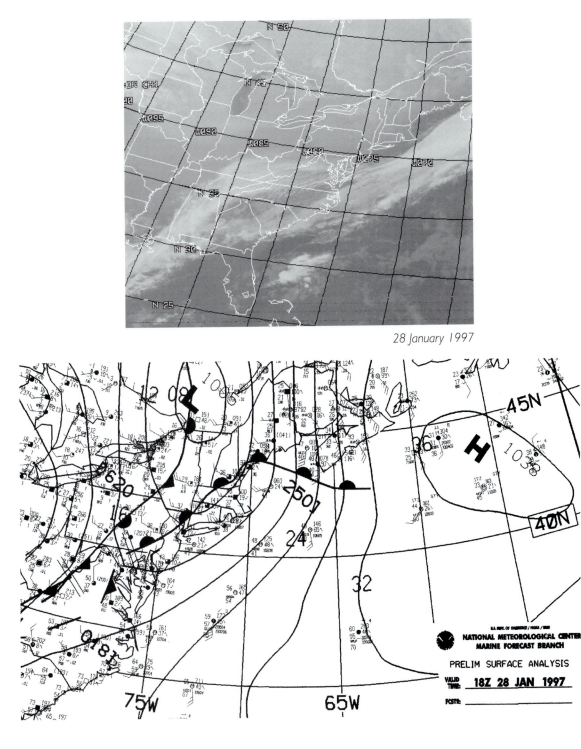

28 January 1997

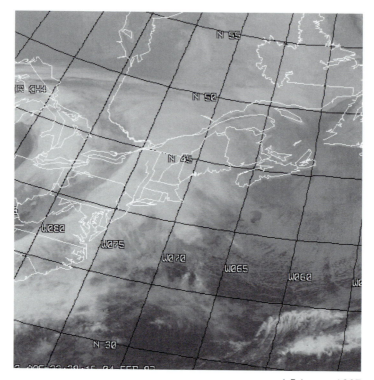

4 February 1997

Three images, a combination of IR and VIS, show low-pressure development on 4, 5, and 6 February 1997. An IR image on 4 February (above) shows low pressure in the west, with counterclockwise spiraling beginning. Note that the geographical gridding is slightly off. Warm low-level clouds (gray in color) are particularly noticeable over the ocean south of Nova Scotia. On the IR image of 5 February (next page, left) the low has now developed a comma shape, and clear air to its west indicates the influx of cold dry air. Finally, on the VIS image on 6 February (next page, right) the low shows bright white, indicating a high level of moisture. Compare the images with the surface analysis chart of 4 February 1997 and the 48-surface forecast for 4–6 February 1997. When correlating satellite images with weather charts it is important to note the locations of fronts and the centers of low and high pressure.

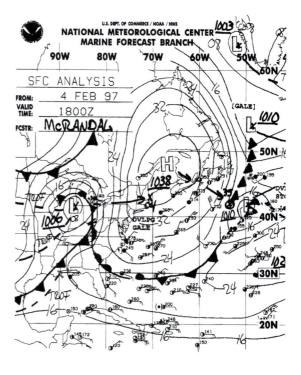

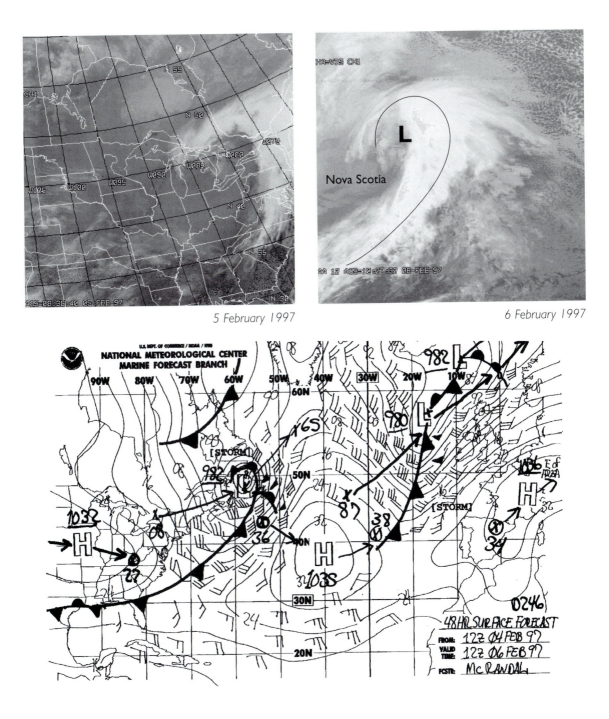

5 February 1997

6 February 1997

Two images, one IR (top) and one VIS (bottom), showing a low-pressure system over the Great Lakes. Note that cloud texture appears on the visible image: visible images show reflected light, and thus reveal shadows and contrasts. On the VIS image, for example, the vertical development of a low-pressure system over the eastern Great Lakes is evident in dense, textured bright white clouds. Likewise, puffy cumulus clouds visible over Florida indicate hot surface temperatures producing rising, convective flow. IR images show just radiated energy, or temperature, so there is no texture. Also note the strong easterly wind flow south of the Great Lakes low, evident as cloud streets.

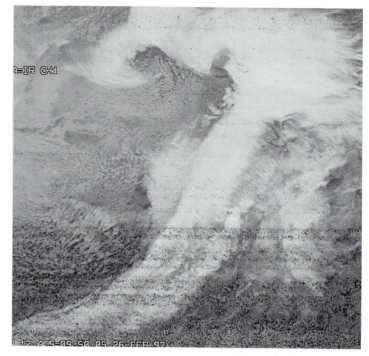

26 February 1997

27 February 1997

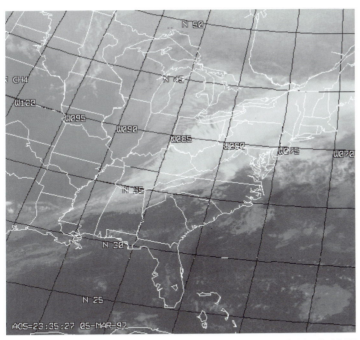

This IR image shows the beginning of low-pressure development, when warm, moist air and cold, dry air are mixing under an upper-level trough. This cloud shape is called a baroclinic leaf, baroclinic referring to an unstable atmosphere and leaf to the cloud's leaf-like shape. This cloud shape is unique to low-pressure system development. The white color of clouds indicates cold temperatures and thus vertical development. Low clouds surrounding the leaf are gray.

5 March 1997

An IR image of an area of low pressure on 31 March 1997. Note the cloud tops being blown off along the cold front, indicating strong upper-level winds. High clouds extend far to the east of the low's center. The associated cold front (highlighted) shows signs of breaking up near its western end, indicated by disconnected and broken clouds, but intense and bright clusters over Florida represent thunderstorm activity.

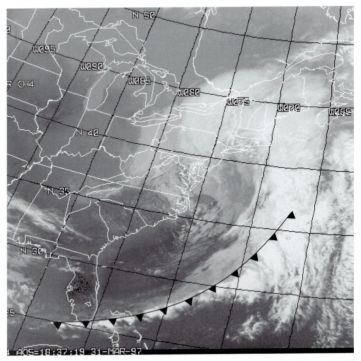

31 March 1997

An IR image (top) and a VIS (bottom) image of a fully developed low-pressure system off the U.S. East Coast on 1 April 1997. The superimposed geographical lines are slightly off. Compare the images, recalling that bright white represents cold on the IR image, and cloud density—and therefore reflectivity—on the VIS image. Note how clouds are aligned with surface wind flow. Clear skies over land indicate cold, dry airflow. The increase in clouds over the Gulf Stream shows where warm, moist air and cold, dry air are mixing, producing condensation. Observe the bands of clouds throughout the low, indicating strong convection, and distinct cloud lines. The low has significant inward spiraling near its center, typical of gale-force and stronger systems. This is a large low, affecting the entire East Coast.

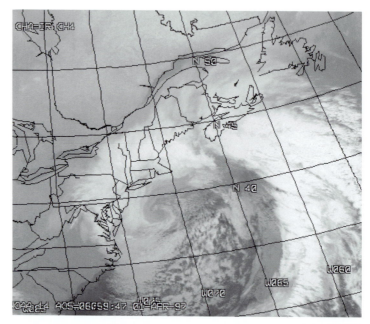

1 April 1997

1 April 1997

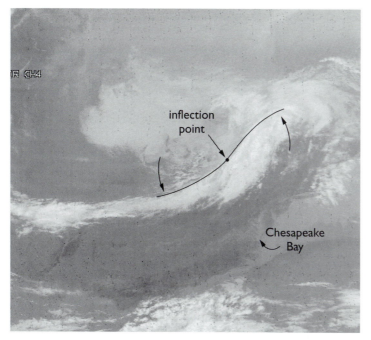

An IR image showing developing low pressure over the Great Lakes region in April. The Gulf Stream is visible with a distinct warm eddy. High, cold clouds are white, while low-level clouds are gray. A dense trailing cold front shows in east-to-west orientation. Clear air north of the cold front is where the strongest jet stream winds are found. Note the convex-concave inflection (highlighted) on the low's backside; an inflection will always appear as the counterclockwise rotation of a surface low begins. Also notice the north wall of the Gulf Stream.

16 April 1997

This IR image shows strong thunderstorm activity over south Florida and the middle United States, visible as very white (cold) clouds, with tops being blown off by upper-level winds. The Gulf Stream current is also visible just off the U.S. East Coast, with shades of gray representing temperature gradients along the west and north walls. The strongest Gulf Stream currents are found where temperature changes rapidly.

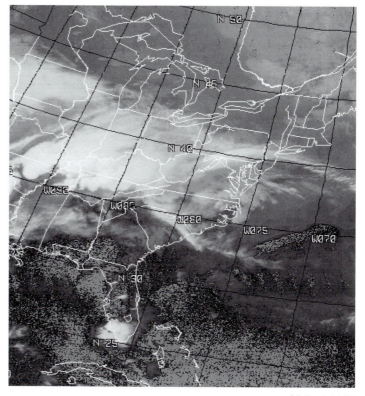

28 April 1997

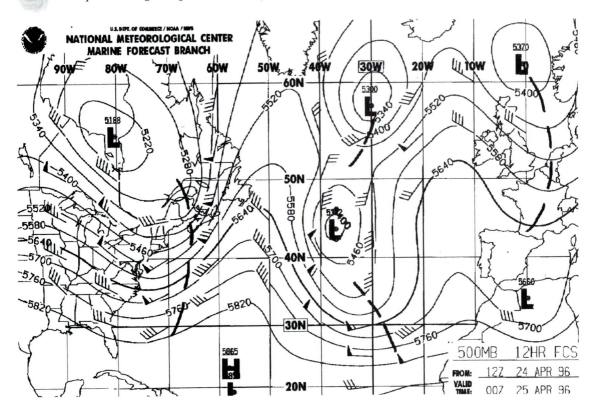

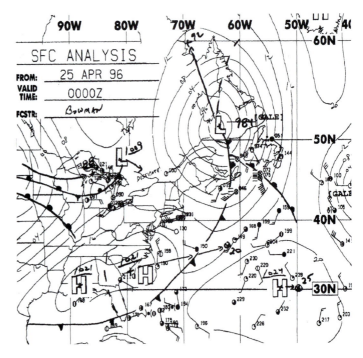

24 April 1996

A large cold front is passing across the U.S. East Coast,
attached to a more northerly low-pressure system. Note
the trough on the 500-mb chart supporting this system.
Wind shifts from southwest to northwest across this cold
front are shown by isobar lines and surface wind arrows.
This is a fast-moving cold front, being pushed along by
50- to 70-knot jet stream winds.

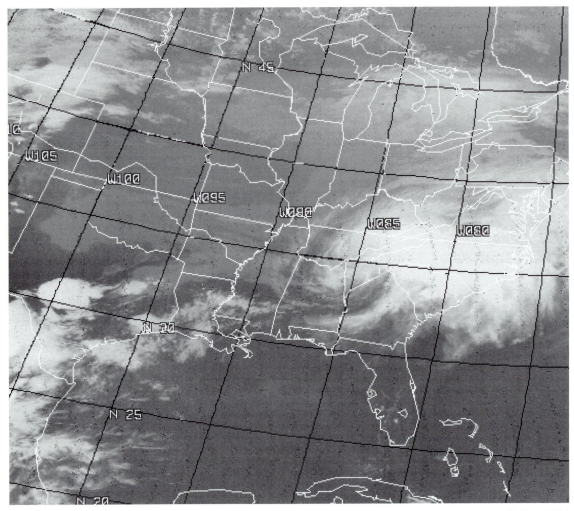

5 May 1996

A low-pressure system is seen developing along a frontal boundary east of Cape Hatteras on the 36-hour surface forecast; an earlier IR image shows the distinctive comma cloud shape and dense central cloud mass north of Florida. Thunderstorms gather over Texas (bright white on the IR image) in the vicinity of a dry line, an area of little moisture and strong thermal pressure gradients that is noted on the North American surface analysis chart (top right). Clear skies over the Gulf of Mexico are associated with a ridge of high pressure extending from Atlantic high pressure.

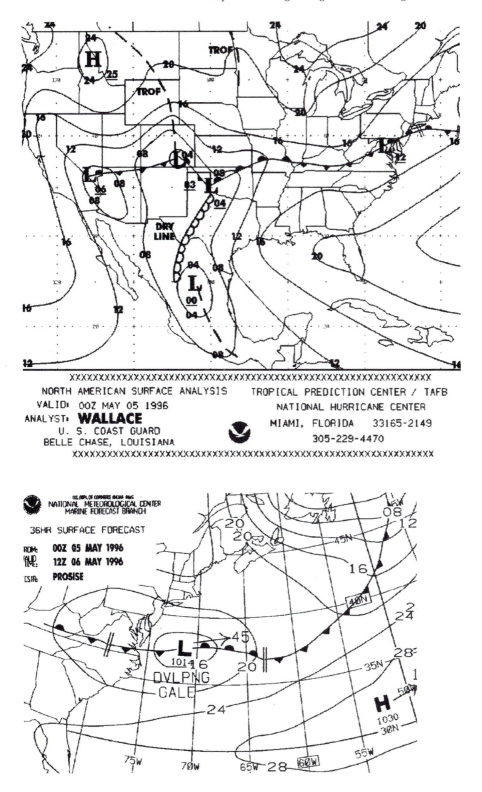

xxxxxxxxxxxxxxxxxxxxxxxxxxxxxxxxxxxxxxxxxxxxxxxxxxxxxxxxxxx
NORTH AMERICAN SURFACE ANALYSIS   TROPICAL PREDICTION CENTER / TAFB
VALID: 00Z MAY 05 1996   NATIONAL HURRICANE CENTER
ANALYST: **WALLACE**   MIAMI, FLORIDA   33165-2149
   U. S. COAST GUARD   305-229-4470
BELLE CHASE, LOUISIANA
xxxxxxxxxxxxxxxxxxxxxxxxxxxxxxxxxxxxxxxxxxxxxxxxxxxxxxxxxxx

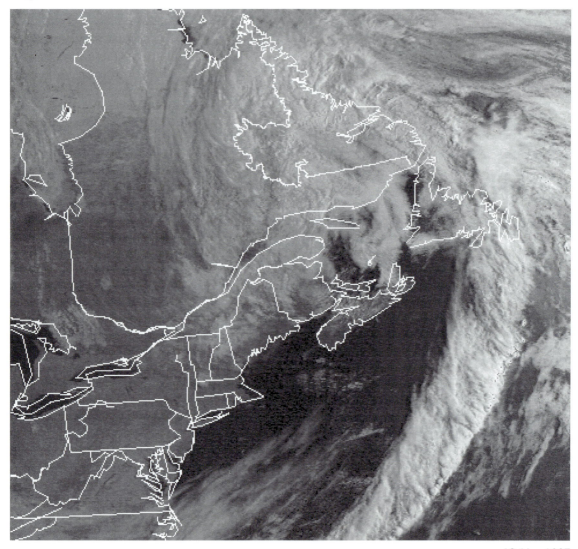

13 May 1997

This is a visible image of a well-developed cold front trailing to the south of a low-pressure center. The pronounced and distinct cloud line at the leading edge of the cold front is a band of strong convection, producing squalls and thunderstorms. This front is several hundred miles wide and indicates a strong low.

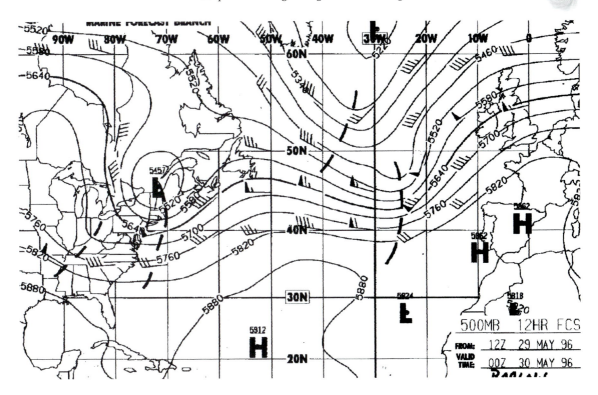

500MB   12HR FCS
FROM: 12Z 29 MAY 96
VALID TIME: 00Z 30 MAY 96

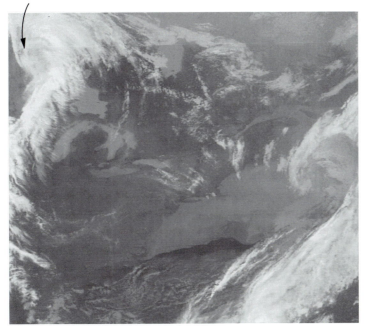

31 May 1996

Two 500-mb troughs support two surface low-pressure systems, with a ridge of high pressure over the U.S. East Coast sandwiched between. A comma cloud is evident to the east of the Atlantic Coast on this IR image from 31 May; a second comma cloud to the west (arrow) is partially obscured. The low indicated on the 500-mb chart of 30 May corresponds to the more easterly low on the IR image; the second low on the IR image developed from the more westerly trough on the 500-mb chart. Clear skies under the ridge of high pressure reveal the Gulf Stream and its eddies. Together, this image and the 500-mb chart illustrate the alternating trough-ridge-trough pattern in weather systems.

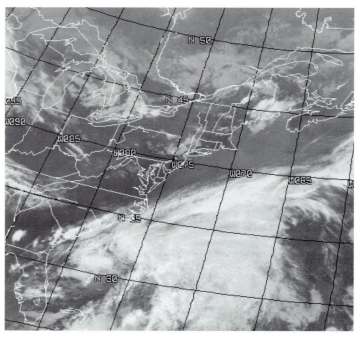

22 May 1996

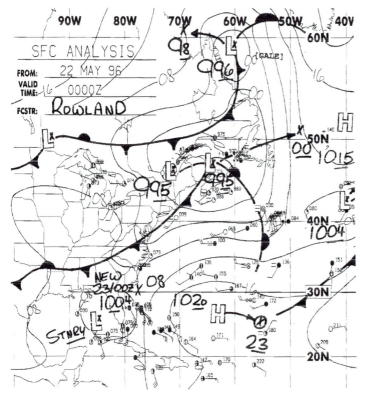

An IR image, a surface analysis chart, and a 500-mb chart combine to show a cloud band along a cold front aligned with the U.S. East Coast. Low pressure is stationary over Florida, and a large dip in the 500-mb contour line over Florida indicates an area of unsettled conditions. Clear air lies to the west of the cold front where cool, dry continental air resides. Warm Gulf Stream waters assist in fueling cloud formation along the coast.

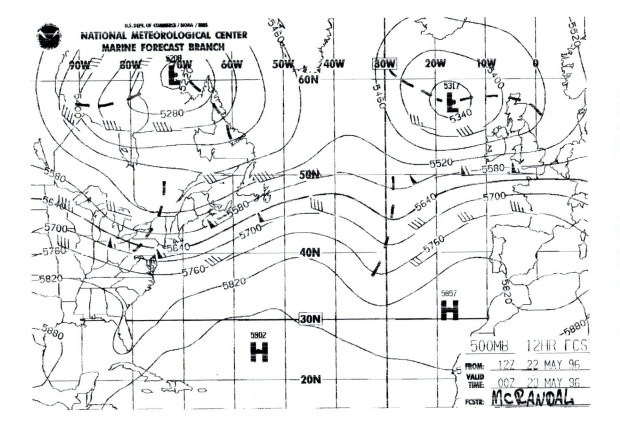

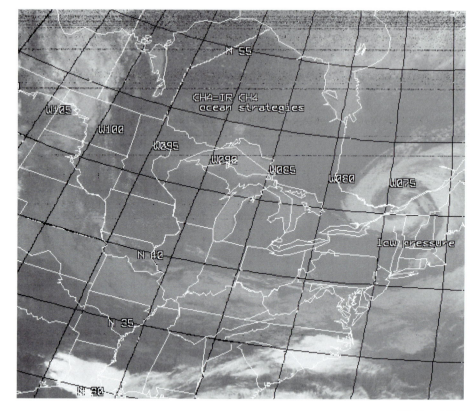

29 May 1996

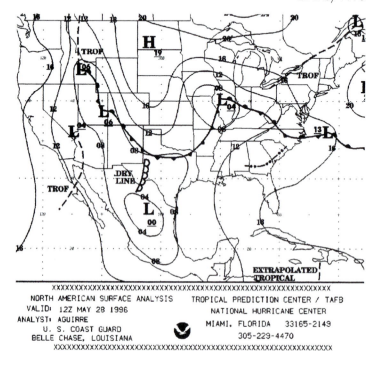

NORTH AMERICAN SURFACE ANALYSIS   TROPICAL PREDICTION CENTER / TAFB

VALID: 12Z MAY 28 1996   NATIONAL HURRICANE CENTER

ANALYST: AGUIRRE

U. S. COAST GUARD   MIAMI, FLORIDA   33165-2149

BELLE CHASE, LOUISIANA   305-229-4470

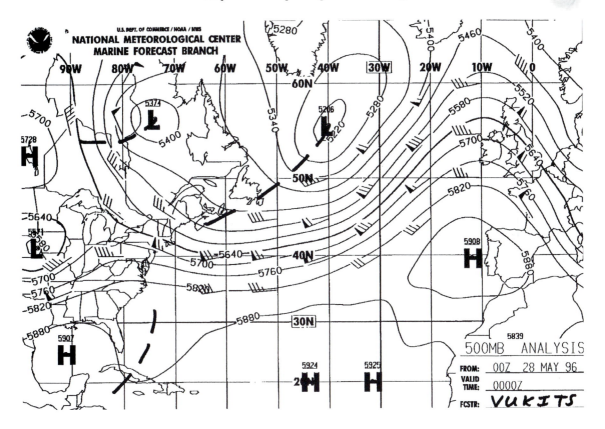

A well-formed low-pressure system over New England is seen on this IR image, supported by an upper-level trough seen on the 500-mb chart. Note the clouds along the mid-Atlantic front and low-level (gray) clouds south of the Great Lakes. A squall line is noted over Georgia on the North American surface analysis chart, as well as a dry line over Texas. Both are areas where strong convective activity can be expected. Notice how strong jet stream winds (50 to 70 knots) are moving weather systems quickly to the east.

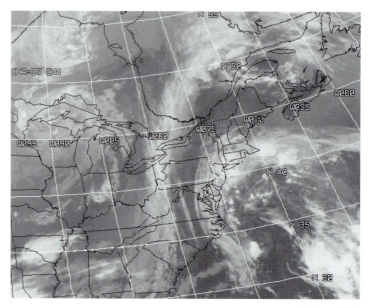

3 June 1996

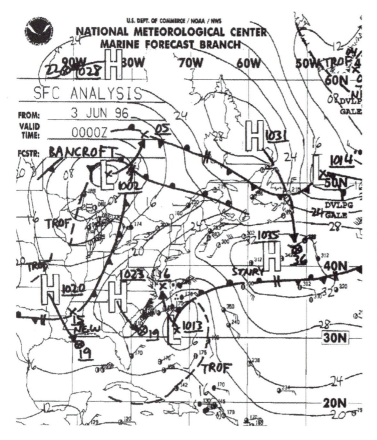

Two IR images on 3 and 4 June show a low-pressure system moving up the U.S. East Coast, with a ridge of high pressure sandwiched between it and a cold front approaching from the west. The low is also shown on a surface analysis chart at 30 north/72 west moving northwest. A multitude of high and low clouds (high, cold clouds appear brighter and low, warm clouds are darker) are to be expected in the summer months, which bring increased heat input into the Northern Hemisphere. Compact and bright white clouds indicate localized thunderstorms. The decreasing resolution of the low in the IR image on 4 June indicates it is weakening. The gridding is slightly off on the 4 June image.

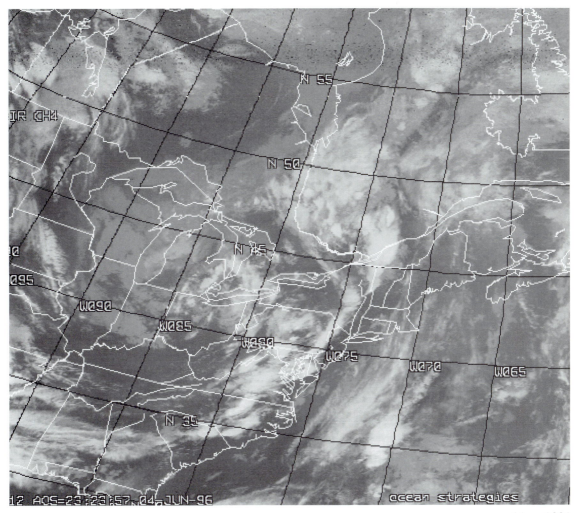

4 June 1996

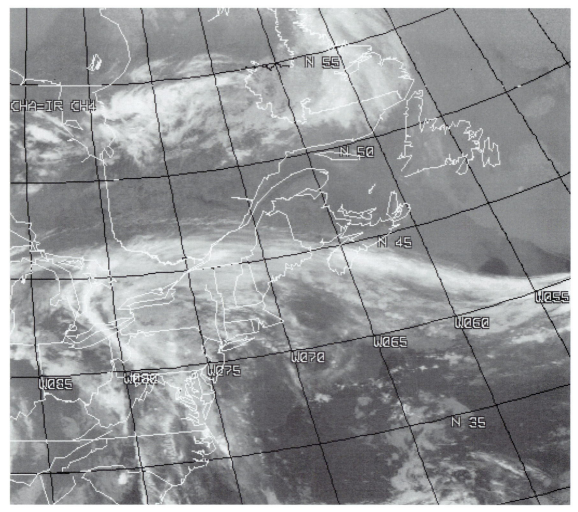

10 June 1996

An IR image, a 500-mb chart, and a surface analysis chart together show the relationship between upper-air flow and cloud formation. Notice that cloud distribution outlines the area of Atlantic high pressure. Dense clouds are associated with the trough south of the Great Lakes on the 500-mb chart, and a band of clouds lies along the area of strongest jet stream movement across Canada and the North Atlantic. A weak comma cloud is associated with the low forming over northern Canada. Areas of isolated clouds and thunderstorms exist elsewhere, as would be expected during June. Fog is present along the New England coast, brought by the stalled front and seen as a low-lying warm cloud on imagery.

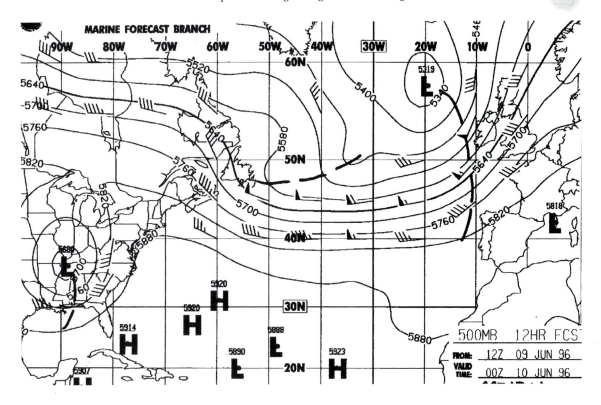

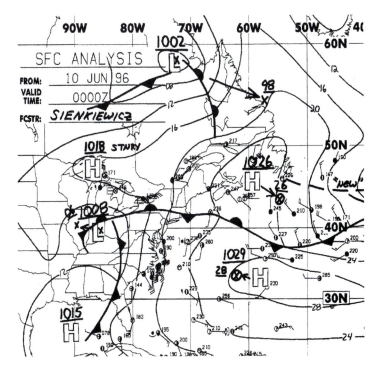

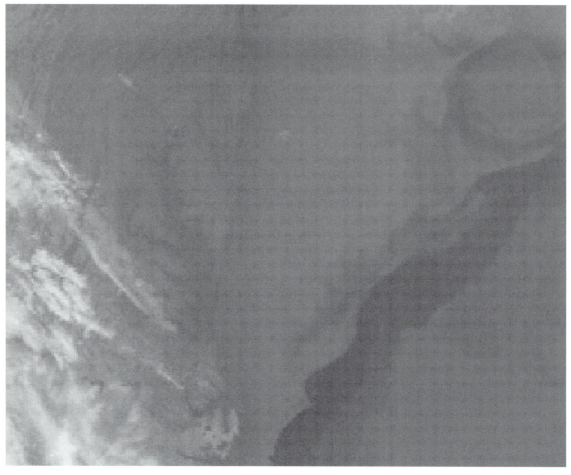

11 June 1997

A strong summer high-pressure system positioned over the U.S. East Coast brought cloud-free skies and permitted capture of this IR image showing a large Gulf Stream warm eddy, as well as the north wall of the Gulf Stream with its graduated temperatures. Temperature gradients are represented by different shades of gray. Note the clouds encroaching from the west, pushing against the high-pressure system's western edge.

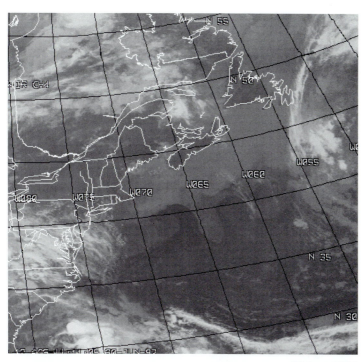

30 June 1997

Two beautifully clear IR images of Gulf Stream and strong summertime convective activity, typical of seasonal thunderstorm activity, offshore near 30 north between 70 and 75 west. Note how the clouds in this area grow in size and brightness between 30 June and 1 July. As this is an IR image, bright white indicates cold and gray-black indicates warm temperatures. Also notice the various shades of gray within the Gulf Stream, indicating changes in water temperature.

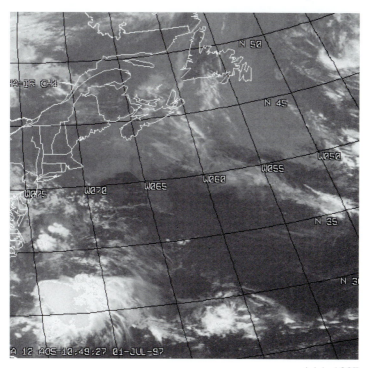

1 July 1997

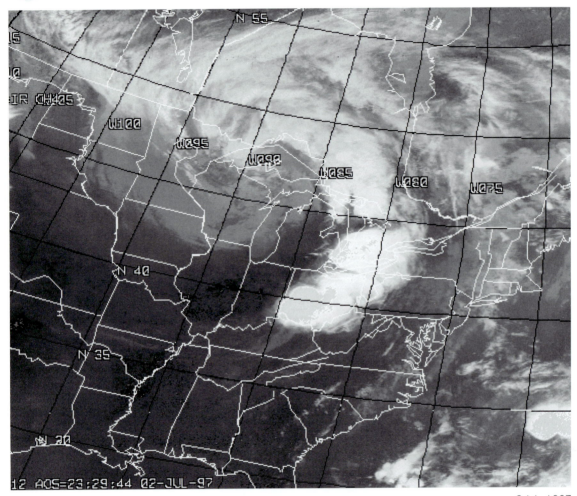

2 July 1997

*This IR image shows a summer low-pressure system over
the Great Lakes with strong convective activity, most likely thunderstorms, just south of Lake Erie. Bright white
indicates high, cold clouds on the IR image; gray clouds
are warm, low-level features. Note how clouds align with
wind flow, counterclockwise around low pressure. Clear
skies over the southern states indicate high pressure.*

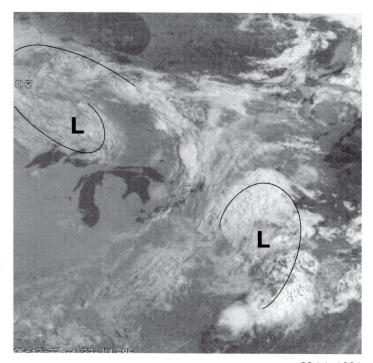

23 July 1996

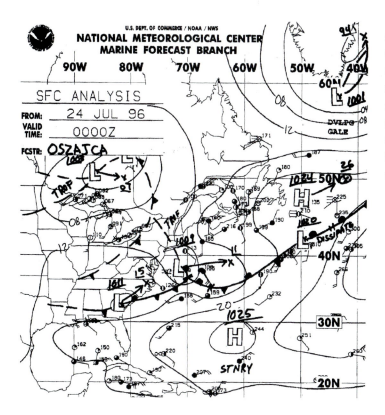

A VIS image captured on 23 July 1996 showing two low-pressure systems developing, one over the Great Lakes and another off the U.S. East Coast. Note the cloud textures and concentration along trough lines, as shown on the surface analysis chart. Lows are moving east, following the jet stream, and staying north of the Atlantic high-pressure area.

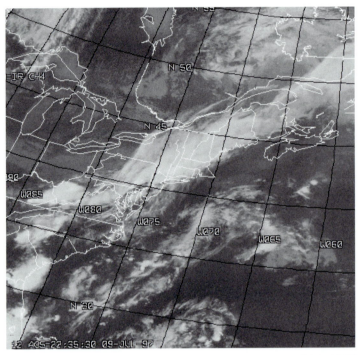

9 July 1997

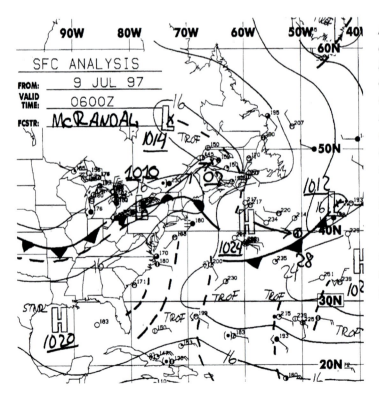

A July low-pressure system developing over New England is seen on this IR image, as well as thunderstorms and clouds along trough lines off the southeast U.S. coast. Note the strong thunderstorm activity in the Florida-Georgia bight on the North American surface analysis chart (corresponding to the trough on the surface analysis) and clear skies over the Great Lakes. An inflection is seen on the backside of the low-pressure system, indicating counterclockwise rotation. This convex-concave shape is always associated with developing low pressure. Also observe clouds along warm and cold front locations.

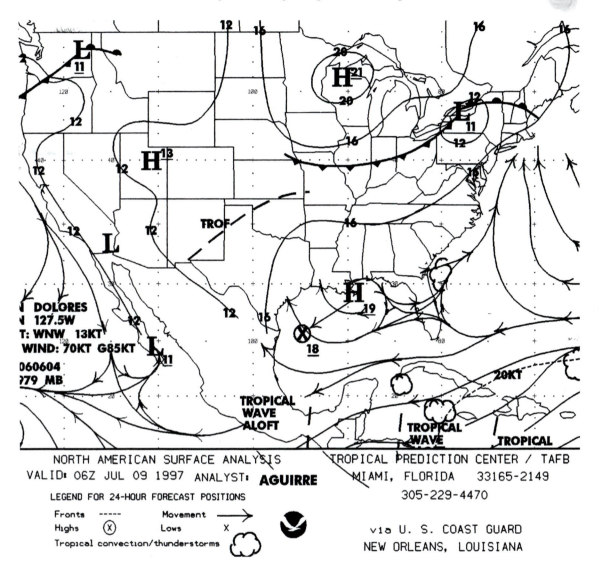

NORTH AMERICAN SURFACE ANALYSIS
VALID: 06Z JUL 09 1997 ANALYST: **AGUIRRE**

LEGEND FOR 24-HOUR FORECAST POSITIONS

Fronts ----   Movement ⟶
Highs   Ⓧ   Lows   X
Tropical convection/thunderstorms

TROPICAL PREDICTION CENTER / TAFB
MIAMI, FLORIDA   33165-2149
305-229-4470

via U. S. COAST GUARD
NEW ORLEANS, LOUISIANA

Hurricane Bertha, with winds of 70 knots and gusts to 85, is shown bearing down on the U.S. East Coast. The VIS image (next page, right) reveals cloud texture and shows a strong cold front north of Bertha. A low over the Great Lakes is also apparent both on the IR satellite images and on the surface analysis charts. Surface and upper-air wind flow is easily determined by examining gray (low, warm) clouds and bright white (cold, cirrus) clouds, respectively. Note the thunderstorms lying along the South Carolina coast, seen as dense and bright white isolated clouds. Bertha does not have a well-defined eye, which is fortunate, as well-defined eyes indicate exceedingly powerful and long-lasting hurricanes.

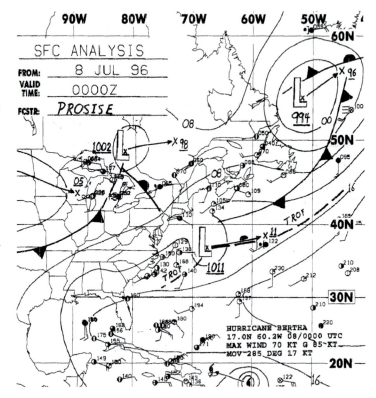

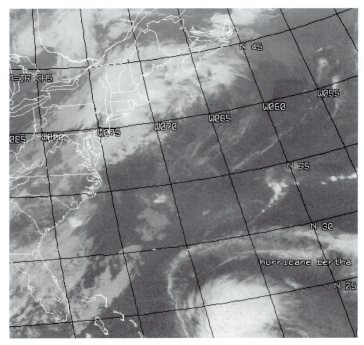

9 July 1996

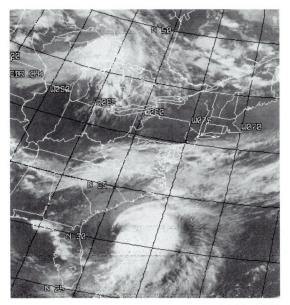

11 July 1996

11 July 1996

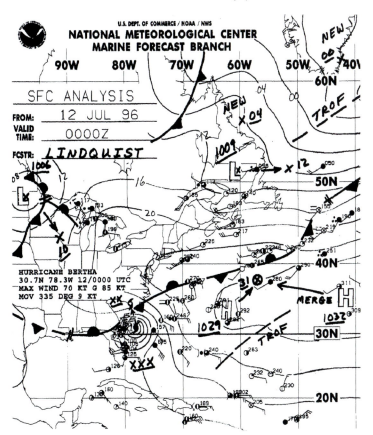

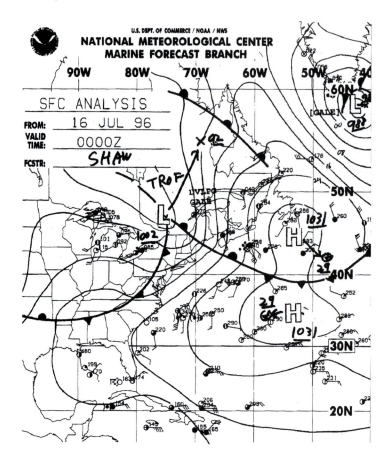

Two separate IR images show low-pressure systems south of Greenland and over Canada in different stages of development. The low near Greenland is fully developed to gale force (top right), as seen by tight and well-defined cloud spirals. The low over Canada is just forming. A bloom of cloud spills over the top of the Atlantic high (A), and clouds off the U.S. East Coast define the edge of the Atlantic high pressure (B). Note the cold front intruding into the Atlantic high, distorting its isobars on the surface analysis chart.

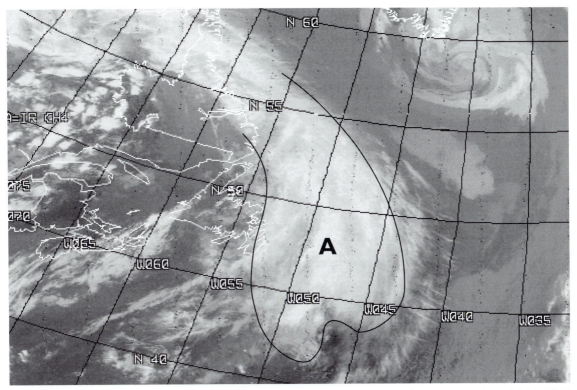

16 July 1996

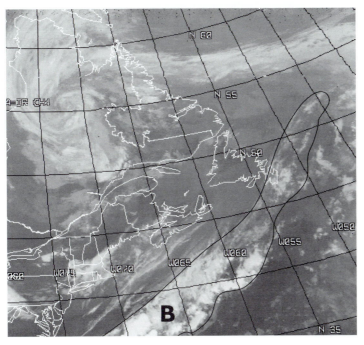

16 July 1996

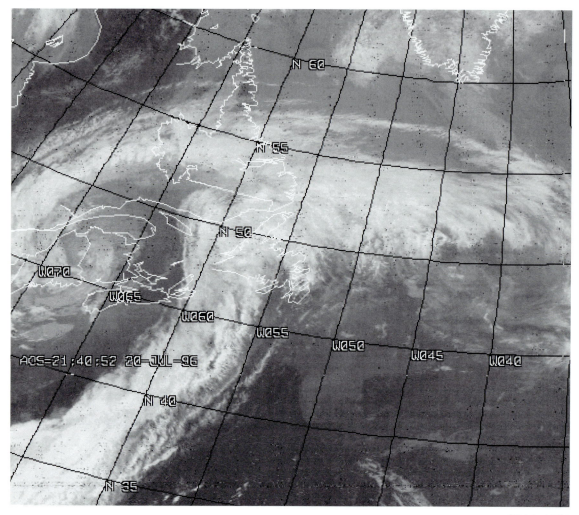

20 July 1996

A well-formed and slow-moving 500-mb trough is supporting this surface low-pressure system, which is showing gale-force winds. The low's center is west of the cold front, allowing an inflow of cold and clear air into the low's center. Isobar lines on the surface chart parallel cloud lines on the IR image. Together the comma cloud, 500-mb trough, and surface frontal pattern show a classic developing low-pressure system.

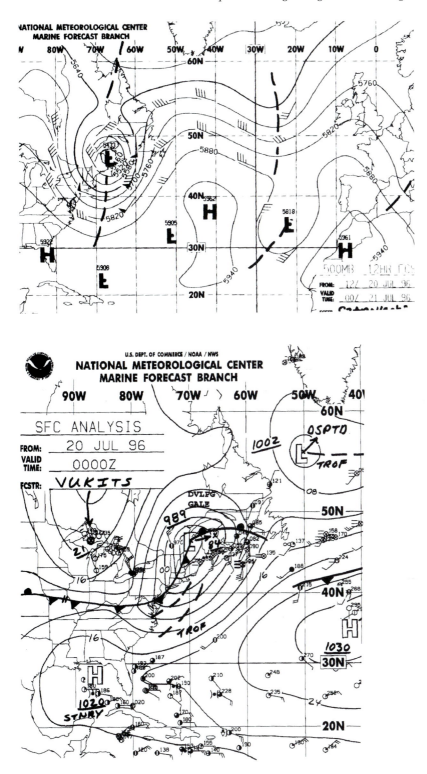

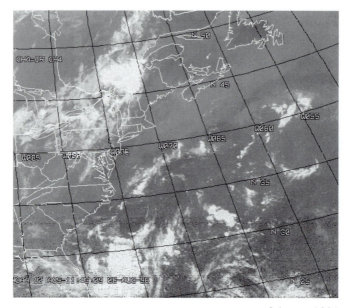

8 August 1996

A dissipating low, with broken and disorganized clouds, is shown east of Cape Hatteras on 8 August, while a new low with tight, dense clouds is forming to the south. Clouds west of New England are associated with an approaching cold front. With its high central pressure and lack of cloud cohesion, this is a good example of the weak low-pressure systems that develop along the perimeter of Atlantic high pressure during the summer months.

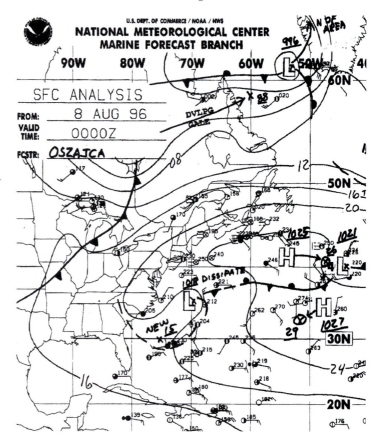

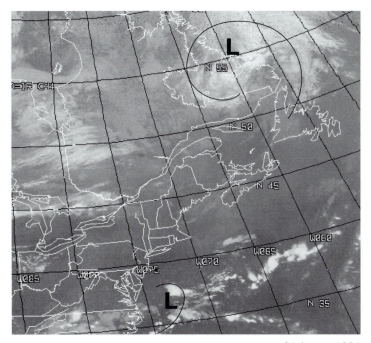

26 August 1996

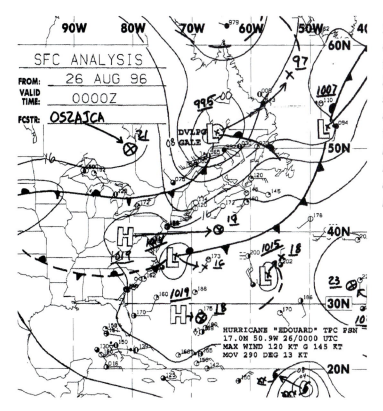

Several low-pressure systems are apparent on this 26 August surface chart, and two appear on the accompanying IR image. One system, with its comma cloud shape, sits over the St. Lawrence Seaway, and another, less intense low is beginning to develop off Cape Hatteras. A pocket of high pressure is over New England and moving east. Hurricane Edouard is shown on the surface chart but is not within the boundaries of the IR image.

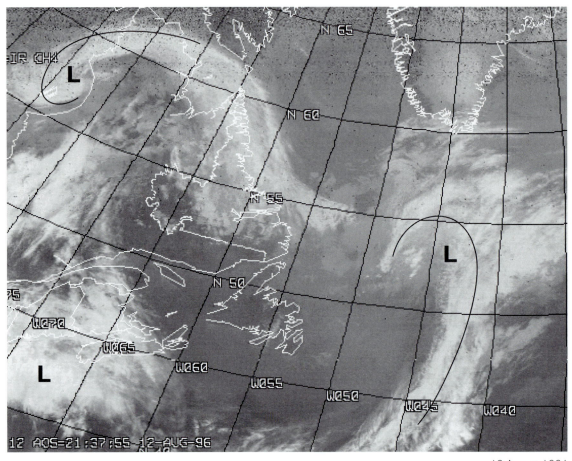

12 August 1996

Three low-pressure systems—two fairly developed and one developing west of Nova Scotia—and an area of high pressure are seen on this IR image. Note how lows and highs are positioned under troughs and ridges shown on 500-mb chart. Each low has a noticeable counter-clockwise wind flow, as revealed by cloud alignment as well as its comma cloud shape. This is a good example of how alternating troughs and ridges in the upper atmosphere influence the development and movement of surface highs and lows.

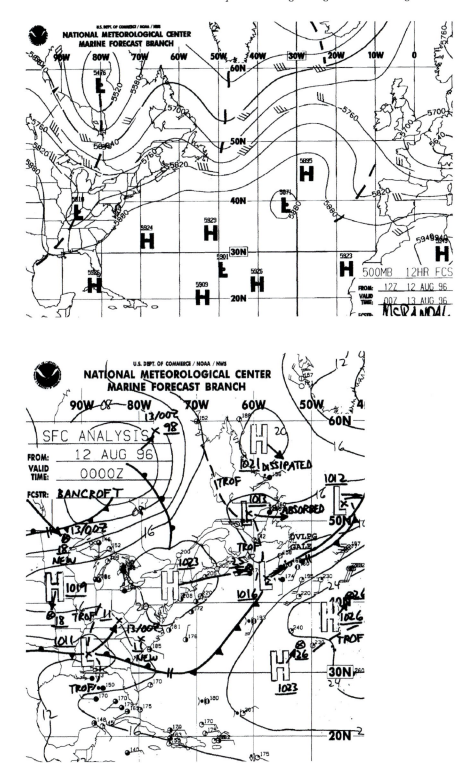

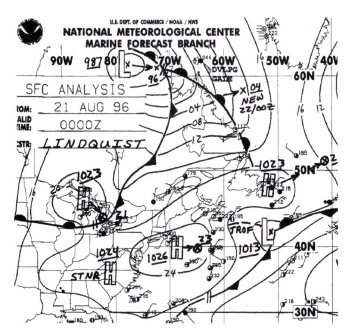

A strong low-pressure system sits over northern Canada while high pressure sits over the U.S. East Coast. This IR image shows a distinct cold front associated with the Canadian low and the comma cloud associated with the low just east of Nova Scotia. Note the clear skies under the centers of highs and cloud bands along their perimeters.

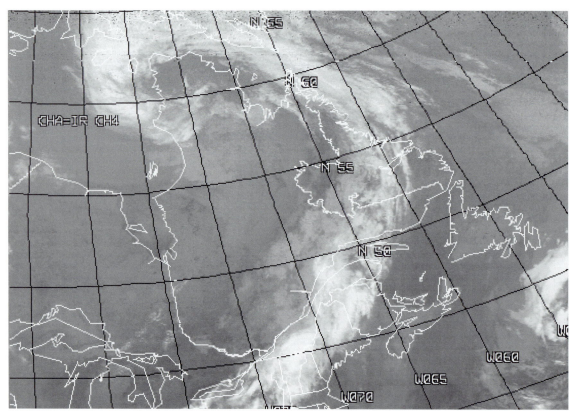

31 August 1996

This VIS image shows a hurricane off the U.S. East Coast and a large high-pressure area over the Great Lakes. Note the shadow cast to the west of the hurricane's towering cloud, and the texture of the hurricane cloud as compared with the flat stratus cloud over the southern U.S. Frequent capture of images such as this are critical to tracking hurricanes and strong low-pressure systems that often move faster than computer models can calculate.

An IR image of a hurricane (bottom) and a VIS image of a low-pressure system (top) along the U.S. East Coast in September. Low, warm (gray) clouds lie south of the low, aligned with wind flow. Both systems have very cold and high clouds, indicating vertical development and intense surface winds.

1 September 1996

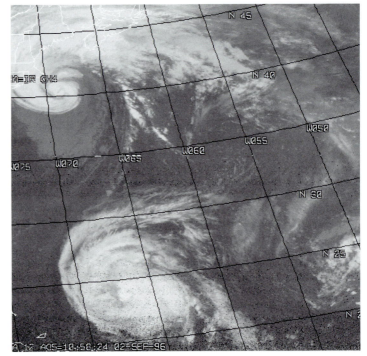

2 September 1996

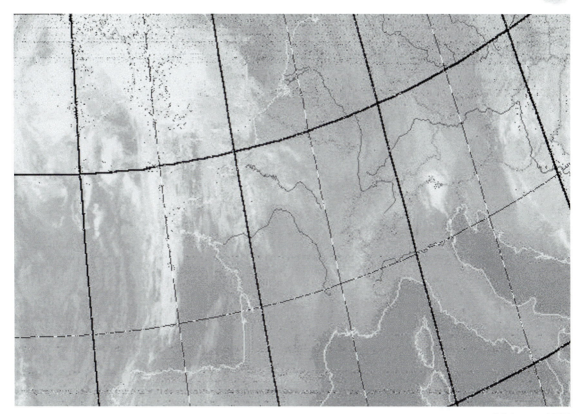

30 August 1997

A strong low-pressure system is making landfall on England's west coast in late August. A distinct cold front is seen in this IR image, with cold temperatures represented by white and warm temperatures by shades of gray and black. Note how the low's center is showing cloud breakup, indicating filling which will lead to dissipation. High pressure with clear skies sits over Italy. The landmass gridding is slightly off in this image.

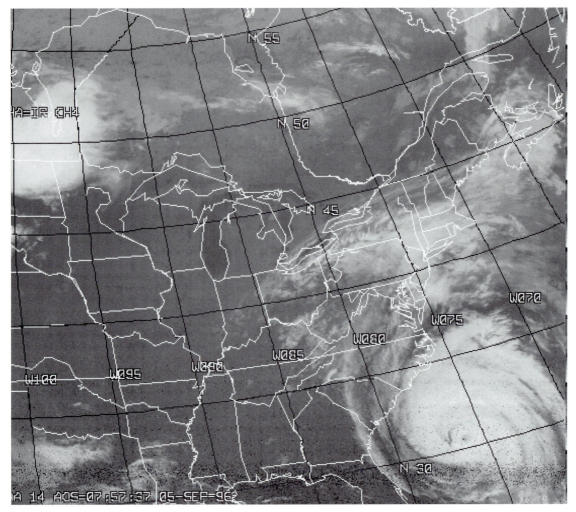

5 September 1996

Hurricane Fran is seen approaching the southeast U.S. coast, with winds at 100 knots and gusts to 120 knots. Several low-pressure systems are also developing to the north off Nova Scotia. Note the position of troughs and ridges on the 500-mb chart and their correspondence with surface systems. High pressure over the middle of the United States is providing clear skies, as seen on the IR image above.

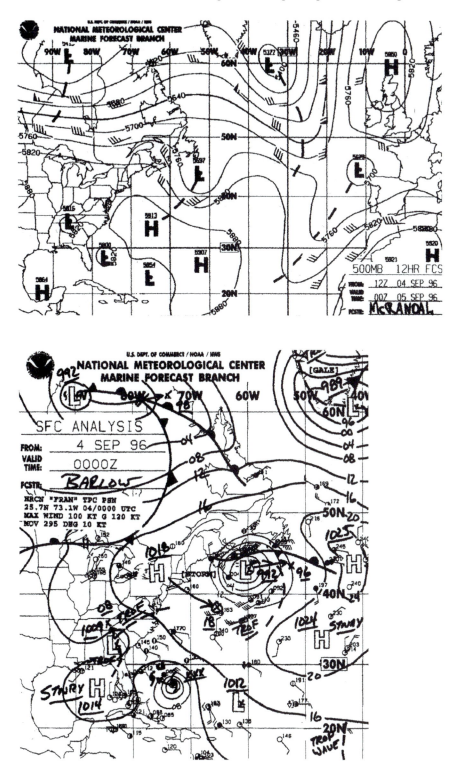

11 September 1996

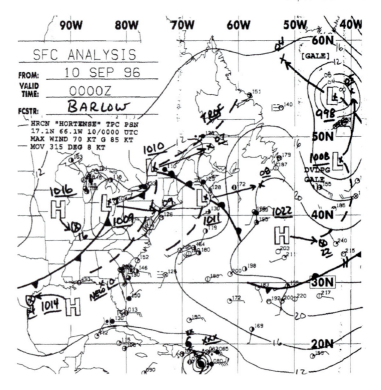

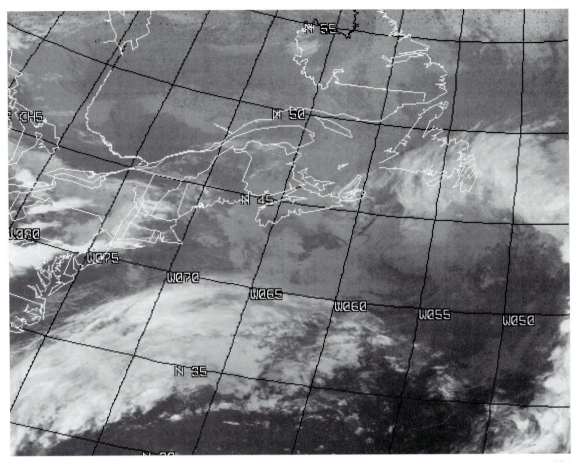

11 September 1996

Hurricane Hortense is seen on a VIS image (top left), and several low-pressure systems to the north are seen on an IR image (above) and a surface chart (left). Hortense has winds to 70 knots with gusts to 85. Note its compact size and lack of the comma cloud shape, distinguishing it from a midlatitude low-pressure system. Several midlatitude lows are moving north of a stationary Atlantic high-pressure area.

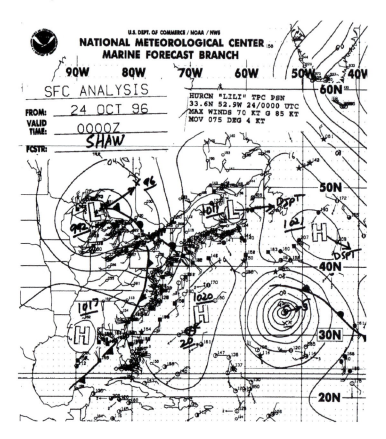

A strong low-pressure system is seen north of the Great Lakes on this IR image and surface analysis chart. Note in particular the "rope cloud" with its cloud tops being blown off near the center of the satellite image. This rope cloud indicates strong convective activity, such as thunderstorms and squalls. Hurricane Lili also appears on the surface chart.

25 October 1996

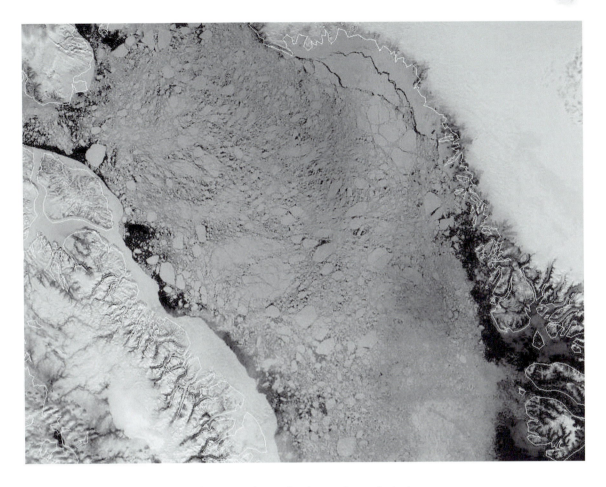

Though not exactly weather, ice can be tracked using satellites just as weather systems are. By combining weather data with information on ice location, thickness, and movement, vessels operating in polar regions can avoid hazardous areas. Canadian and U.S. icebreakers are able to operate year round using a combination of satellite imagery, electronic charting, and weather imagery.

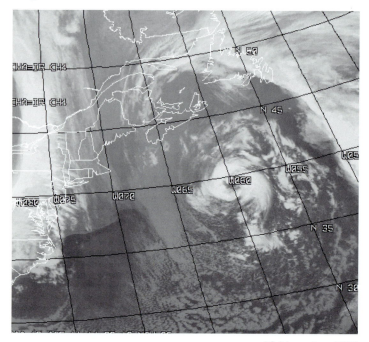

A strong low-pressure system is stalled off the U.S. East Coast under an upper-level trough, as seen in this IR image and the accompanying 500-mb chart. The low's center is near 40 north/60 west. Low-level warm clouds are seen as gray and high, cold clouds as white. Note how the low's cold front is removed from the low's center, revealed on both the IR image and the 24-hour surface forecast chart. A new low is developing along the U.S. East Coast, while large seas exist along the Gulf Stream's north wall, as shown by the cross-hatched area on the 36-hour wind/wave forecast. The Gulf Stream's location is revealed by contrasting gray colors on the IR image.

18 November 1996

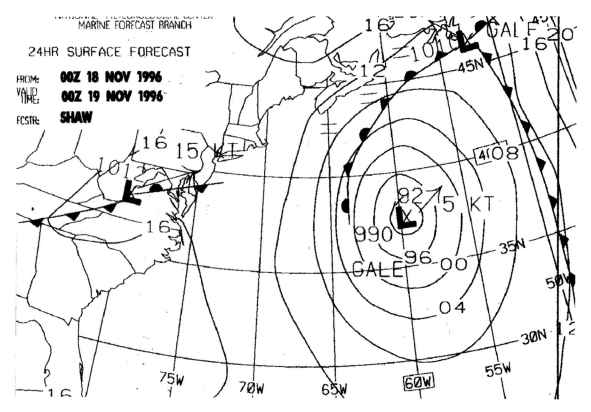

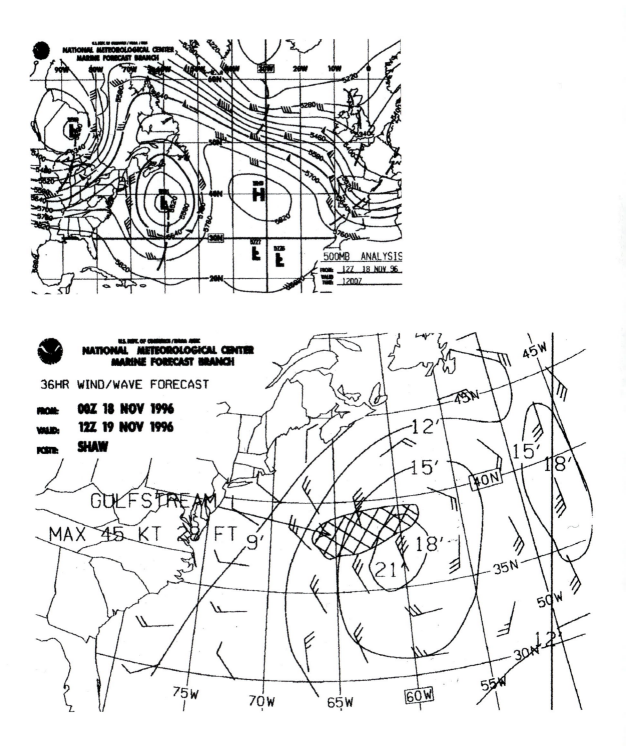

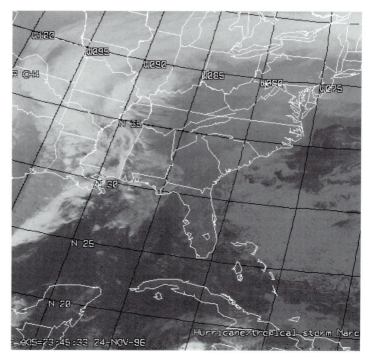

Tropical storm Marco is just visible at the bottom edge of this IR image. Its location is shown on the tropical surface analysis chart. Notice the cold front coming across the Gulf of Mexico and clear skies under the Atlantic high-pressure system.

24 November 1996

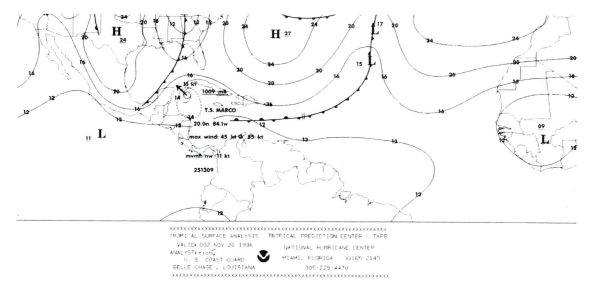

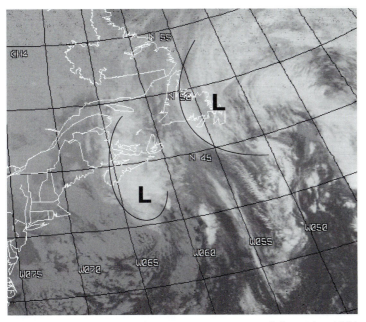

An IR image and a surface analysis chart show the development of two connected low-pressure systems. Note the center of the lows by comparing the latitude and longitude coordinates from the surface chart with the IR image. As lows develop, surface flow is revealed through cloud development, particularly cloud streets and bands near their centers. When two lows develop near each other, they often begin acting as one large low, with both centers rotating counterclockwise around a central point.

5 December 1996

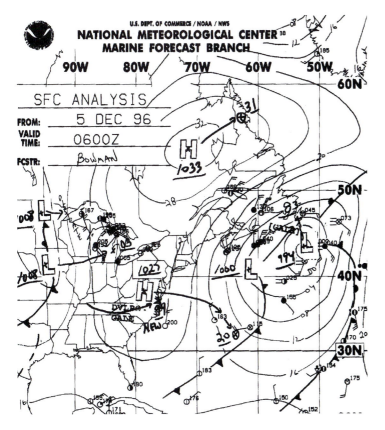

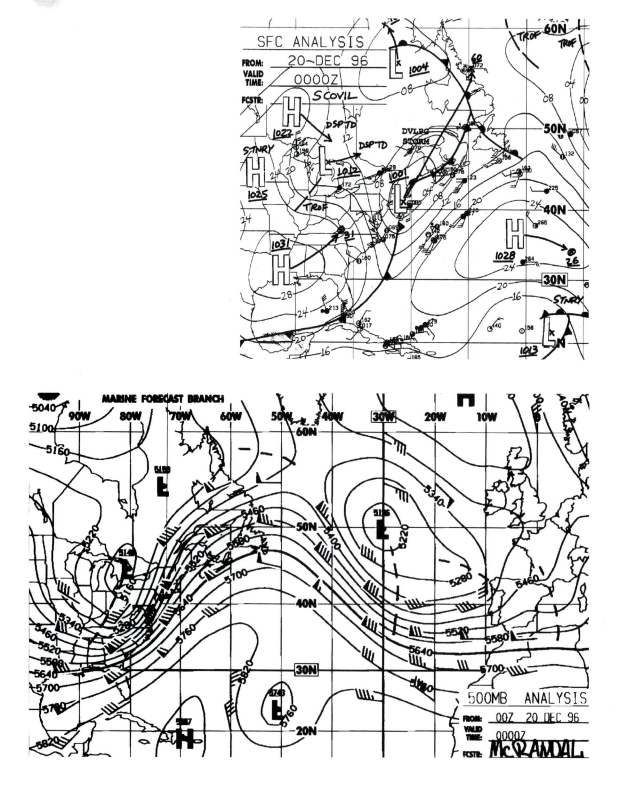

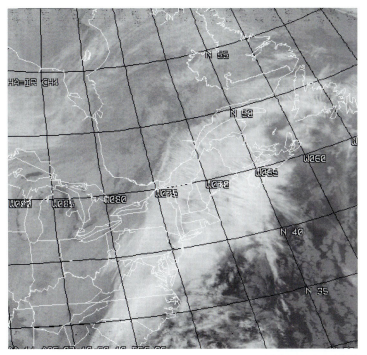

19 December 1996

These two IR images and the accompanying surface analysis and 500-mb charts show development of a storm along the U.S. East Coast. Note how the low forms under the 500-mb trough and then moves northeast, following the upper-air flow pattern. Jet stream winds as strong as 125 knots are shown, which quickly move the low to the northeast while also speeding its intensification. Notice how the low's initial cloud shape conforms to the 500-mb trough shape, with a pronounced north–south orientation. A baroclinic leaf shape is obvious in the 19 December image.

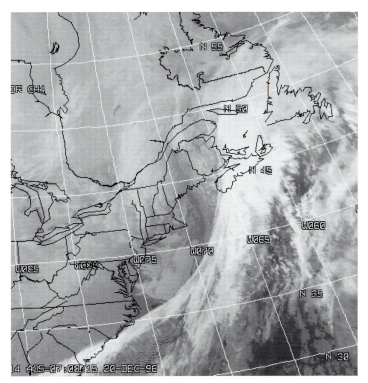

20 December 1996

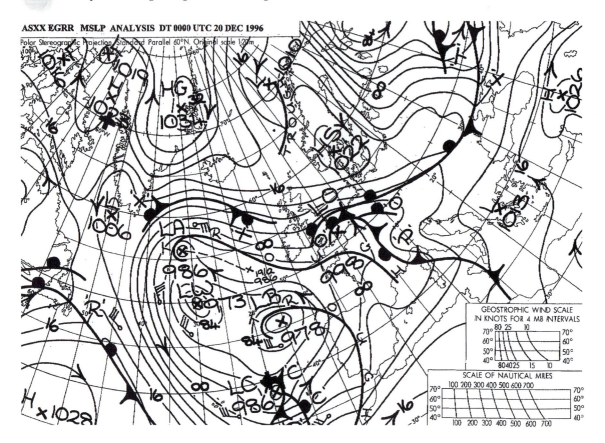

ASXX EGRR MSLP ANALYSIS DT 0000 UTC 20 DEC 1996

Polar Stereographic Projection Standard Parallel 60°N. Original scale 1:20m.

A British surface analysis chart for 20 December 1996,
showing standard weather features: the centers of highs
and lows, fronts, isobars, and wind barbs. Note the
geostrophic wind diagram located at the bottom right
corner of chart. Also examine two areas of low pressure
in close proximity near the center of the chart. A trough
of low pressure exists between these lows, as common
isobar lines bind their centers.

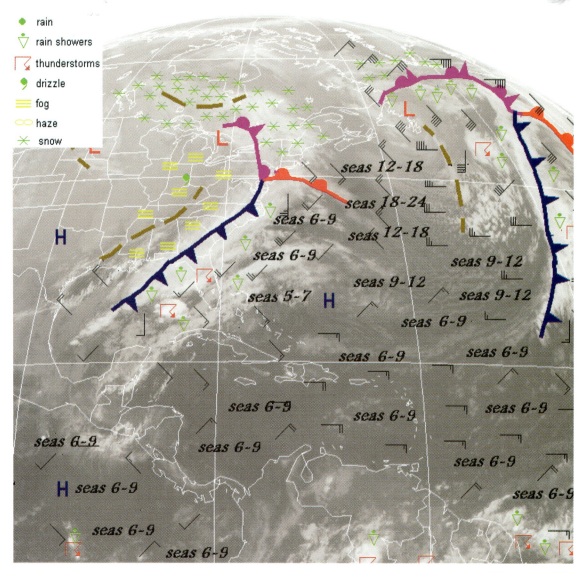

rain
rain showers
thunderstorms
drizzle
fog
haze
snow

4 December 1997

An example of annotated satellite imagery available on the Internet. Here a geostationary IR image has been overlaid with surface features, such as fronts, troughs, precipitation, and sea conditions. When this type of imagery is compared with surface forecasts and 500-mb charts, a complete weather picture emerges.

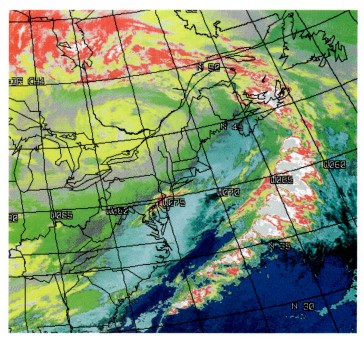

A color-enhanced IR image and a 96-hour surface forecast show a developing low-pressure system. Red represents cold temperatures and outlines the counterclockwise shape of the developing low; patches of white and gray within areas of red represent extreme cold. Areas of high pressure are essentially cloud-free, with only scattered low-level warm clouds showing. This is an example of classic low-pressure system development and movement.

6 January 1996

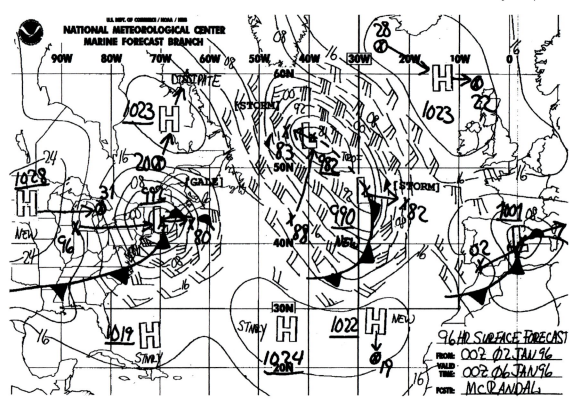

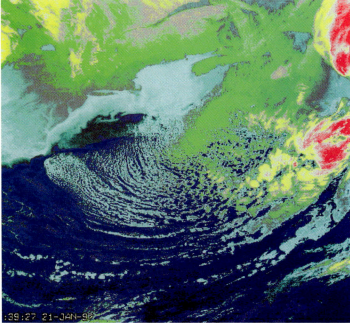

This IR image reveals distinctive cloud streets and westerly wind flow associated with the backside of a low-pressure system. Red shows high (cold) clouds and green-blues show low-level warmer clouds. A strong low has passed off to the east. Land is gray, with Nova Scotia, Long Island, Cape Cod, and the Gulf Stream clearly visible. The strongest Gulf Stream currents will be found where the temperature gradients are steepest. Compare cloud streets, wind flow, and cloud cover with the surface analysis chart of 21 January 1997.

21 January 1997

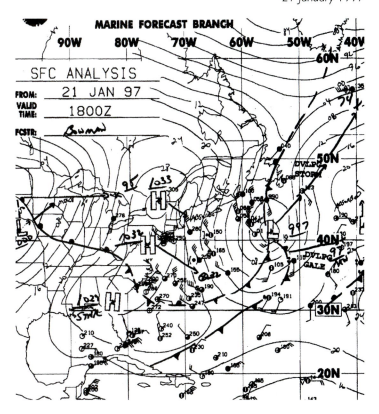

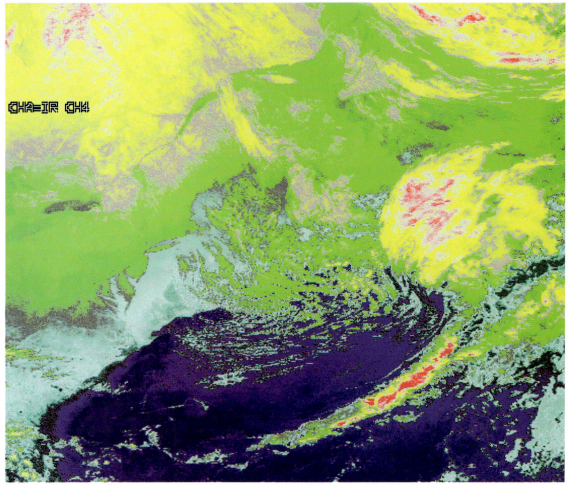

12 March 1997

This color IR image of a March low-pressure system uses red to show cold temperatures and greens and blues for warm. Note the pockets of developed clouds in a cold front indicated by red, as well as the cold clouds in the low's center, also red. The U.S. East Coast appears gray, indicating its warm temperature. The Gulf Stream and its north wall (edge) show clearly. This low-pressure system is still maturing, developing a spiral shape and a distinct comma cloud.

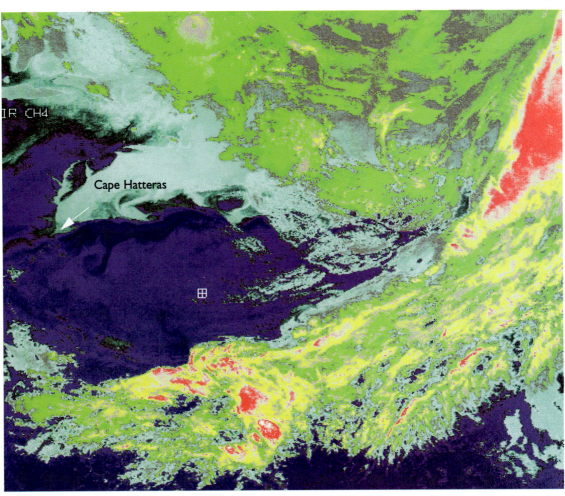

IR CH4

Cape Hatteras

27 March 1997

A color-enhanced IR image with cold temperatures represented by red and warm colors by blue; a standard color palette used on IR images when locating cold clouds is a priority. Note the tail end of a cold front at the upper right and warm Gulf Stream waters with eddies off the U.S. East Coast. Pockets of high, cold clouds are seen at the trailing end of the cold front. Note also how the cold front has bands and pockets of warm and cold clouds.

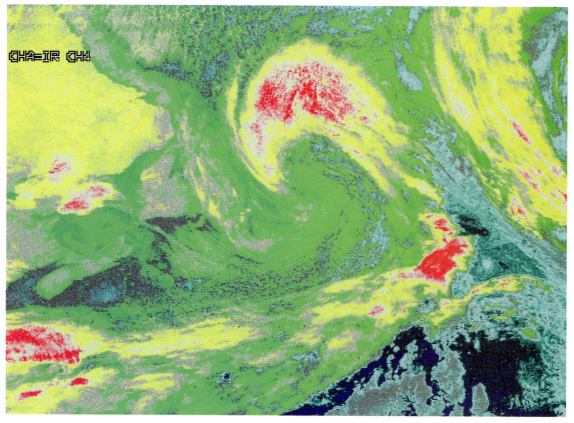

19 March 1997

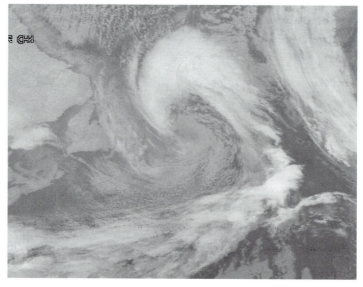

19 March 1997

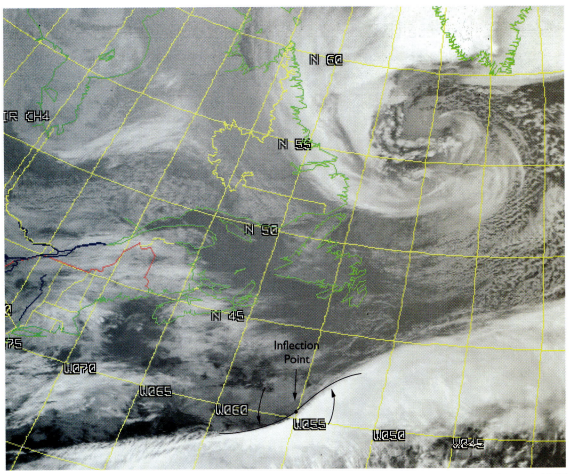

20 March 1997

Three IR images, in both gray scale and color, of a March low-pressure system located between Newfoundland and Greenland. Clouds are aligned with wind flow, and cumulus cloud streets on the low's south side indicate mixing of cold and warm air. The large cloud band to the low's south marks the southern extent of jet stream flow and indicates the boundary between Bermuda-Azores high pressure and low pressure. Note the inflection in this cloud band, a prime location for a secondary low to develop. Numerous clouds indicate extensive atmospheric mixing and presence of moisture.

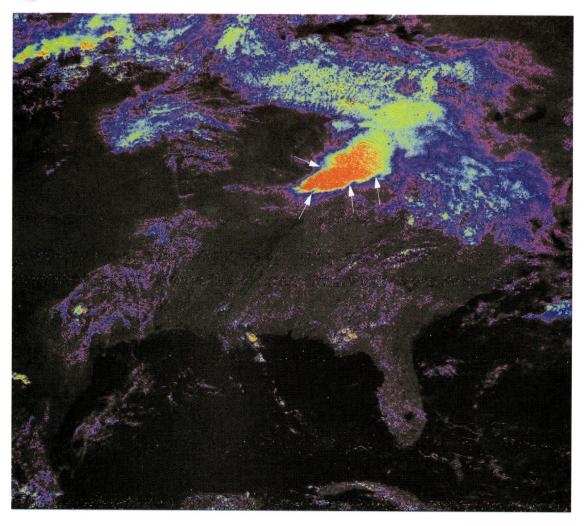

Strong thunderstorm activity, which may not be shown on synoptic weather charts, lies under clouds with cold tops, indicated here in red. Distinctive notches in these clouds (arrows) mark the locations of strongest activity, where tornadoes and downbursts are most likely to occur.

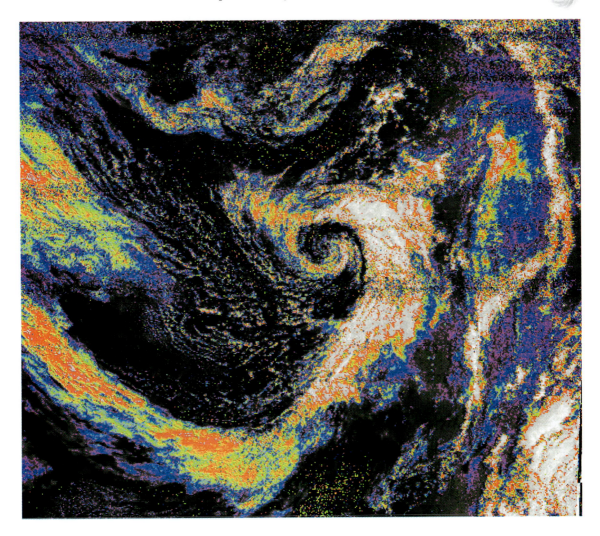

An IR image of developed low-pressure systems, with red and orange representing the coldest cloud top temperatures. Note the symmetrical counterclockwise inward spiral. Middle and low-level clouds are aligned with wind flow in cloud streets.

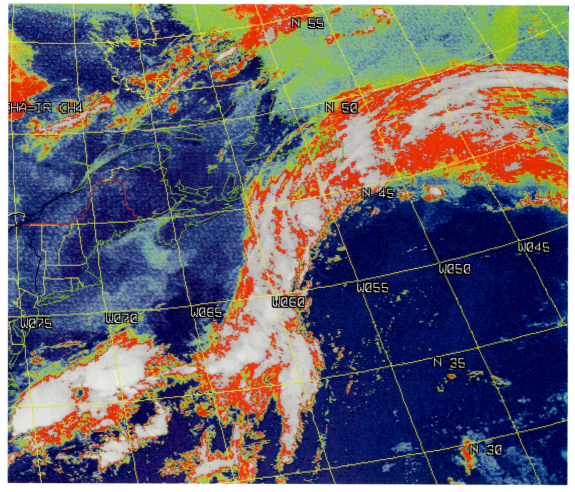

5 August 1996

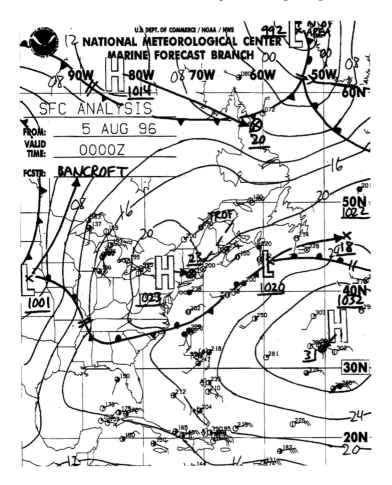

The IR image, surface analysis chart, and 500-mb chart show a cloud band lying along a frontal boundary between two high-pressure systems. Note how clouds conform to the shape of the front and neatly outline the top edge of Atlantic high pressure.

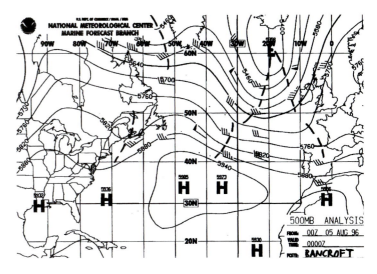

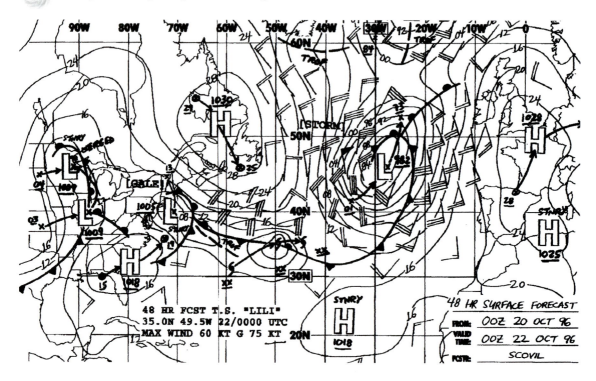

48 HR FCST T.S. "LILI"
35.0N 49.5W 22/0000 UTC
MAX WIND 60 KT G 75 KT

48 HR SURFACE FORECAST
FROM: 00Z 20 OCT 96
VALID TIME: 00Z 22 OCT 96
FCSTR: SCOVIL

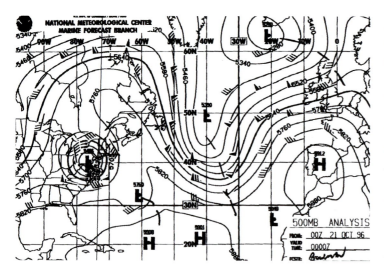

500MB ANALYSIS
FROM: 00Z 21 OCT 96
VALID TIME: 0000Z
FCSTR: Boudman

A stalled low-pressure system over the U.S. East Coast and the slow-moving hurricane Lili are shown acting together to bring torrential rains to the New England coast. Note on the 500-mb chart how an upper-level trough has broken off from the main jet stream flow and is sitting over New England. Also note on the surface chart the stalled front connecting Lili and low pressure, enabling moisture to flow into the low. Successive IR images show the cloud band connecting the two systems slowly weaken from 20 to 21 October 1996. This is an excellent example of how two systems can join together and reinforce each other, producing effects that otherwise would not be felt.

19 October 1996

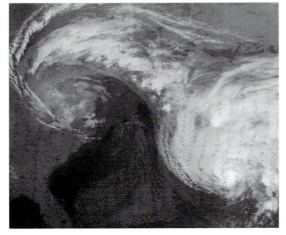

20 October 1996

21 October 1996

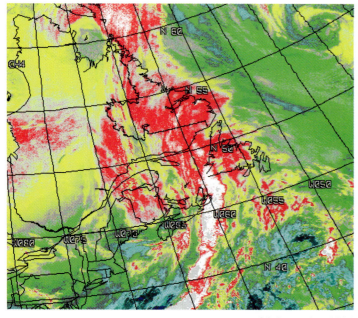

This IR image, captured on 30 December 1996, is displayed with and without color enhancement and shows the beginnings of a rapidly intensifying low-pressure system off the U.S. East Coast. Warm clouds appear blue, cold clouds appear red, and patches of gray and white within areas of red represent extreme cold. Extensive areas of red indicate widespread vertical development. Note the size of the seas south of Nova Scotia on the 24-hour wind/wave chart—24 feet! Also notice the remains of another low in the upper right corner of both images.

30 December 1996

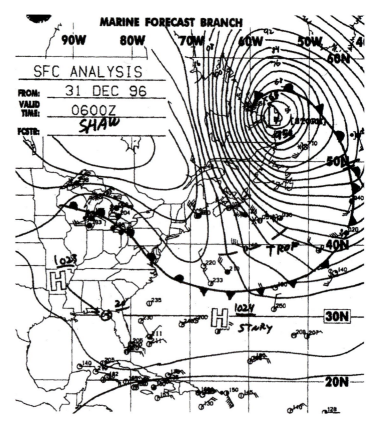

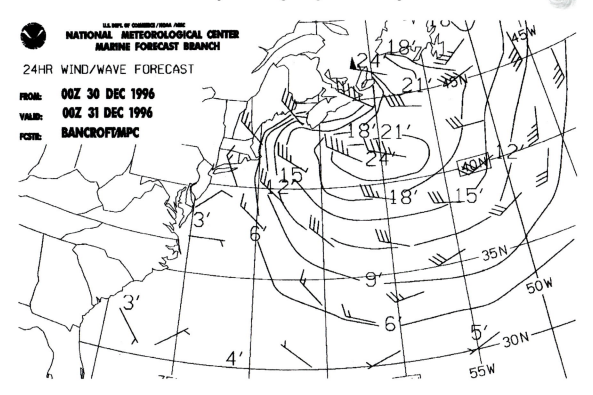

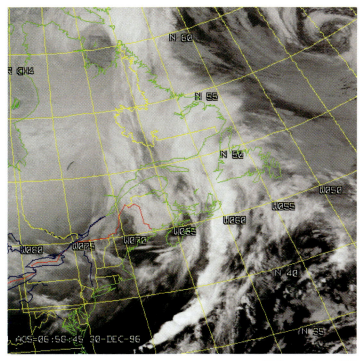

30 December 1996

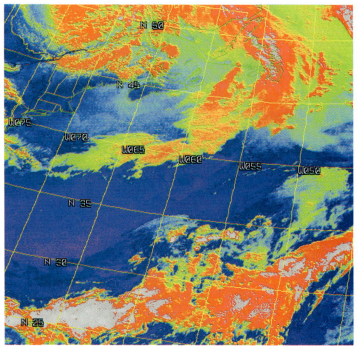

A low-pressure system lies under an upper-level trough near Nova Scotia, as shown on this color-enhanced IR image and the 500-mb chart. Note that the 500-mb storm track line (5,640 contour) lies south of Nova Scotia, indicating that strong lows will form to the north, as this low has done. Scattered and presently unorganized clouds lie along a front to the low's south.

24 May 1996

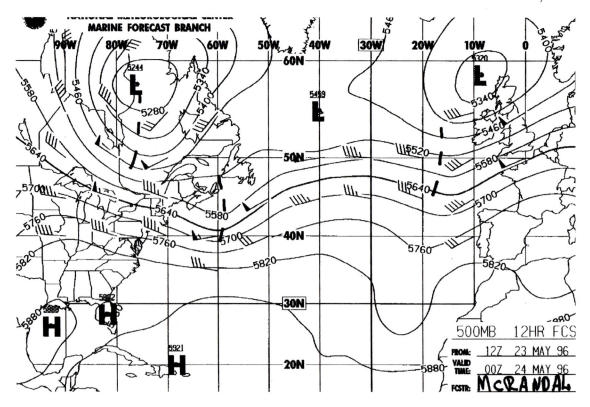

500MB   12HR FCS

FROM: 12Z 23 MAY 96
VALID TIME: 00Z 24 MAY 96
FCSTR: McRANDAL

APPENDIX
1

RADAR USE IN WEATHER

RADAR OPERATION

Radar (for radio detection and ranging) operates by transmitting hundreds or thousands of electromagnetic pulses per second from a rotating antenna. When a reflective object bounces back a pulse, its range can be determined by measuring the time it takes for the echo to return to the antenna (pulses travel at the speed of light). The bearing of the object can also be determined based on the position of the rotating antenna when transmitting and receiving. Ranges obtained from radar are very precise, allowing distances to be measured in increments of yards. Bearings to contacts are less accurate due to the beamwidth of the pulse, which limits target resolution and definition. This spread in bearing is normally less than three degrees, making radar bearings useful but not optimal for navigational purposes.

RADAR CONTROLS

Proper use of radar controls is important, since they affect the detection and resolution of contacts. Following is a list of controls found on most radar sets and a brief description of how each works.

◆ **Precipitation clutter or FTC (fast time constant)** shortens echoes on the display screen and reduces the sensitivity of radar. It is useful for reducing return from local rain showers or squall lines.

◆ **Sea clutter or STC (sensitivity time control)** is used to remove sea clutter at close range. This function should be slowly increased as seas increase; if set too high, sea clutter will wash out targets.

◆ **Gain** should be adjusted whenever range is changed. Improved reception of distant targets and increased brightness may obscure nearby targets. Gain and sea clutter controls should be adjusted together.

- **Tuning** should be set for greatest return when all clutter-suppressing controls are turned down. On many units this adjustment occurs automatically when the radar is turned on.
- **Brilliance** merely controls the brightness of the image on the radar screen and has no effect on reception.
- **Range selector** allows the user to select the area covered on a radar's display. Selecting a certain range does not guarantee that a target will be detected, only that it will be displayed if detected. The smaller the range, the greater the detail of a target.
- **Interference rejection (IR)** is used to remove interference caused by energy from other radar sets operating nearby.

Radar normally operates in two frequency bands, 10 cm (S-band) and 3 cm (X-band). Short, rapid pulses (X-band) provide good definition of targets at close range. Longer, more powerful pulses (S-band) are used to locate weak targets at long range. A typical radar set automatically switches wavelength based on the range selected. When studying approaching weather on radar it is useful to know at what range these frequency changes occur.

When tracking an approaching system on radar, note distinctive or prominent weather features and follow their progress. This will help to preserve continuity as the weather picture evolves and make it easier to recognize new features on radar. As a new feature appears, monitor a previous front or cloud edge for reference. Shifting from one set of features to an entirely different set without overlap increases the chances of misidentification and confusion.

USING RADAR FOR DETECTING SQUALLS AND FRONTS

Radar beams reflect well off water molecules such as rain, so dense frontal system clouds and isolated squalls appear vividly on a radar screen. For radar to be effective in weather analysis, the rain clutter (FTC) and sea clutter (STC) controls—used to eliminate rain and sea surface return in normal use—must be turned off, thus allowing rain and low-level clouds to appear. To improve signal return on a radar screen, the gain control should be increased above normal settings. Gain is often controlled automatically, so a manual override may be required to obtain the desired picture.

In addition to a cloud's density, its shape will give an indication of the severity of an approaching weather system. Although clouds viewed on radar appear in many shapes and orientations, hook (or spiral) clouds and V-notch clouds in particular

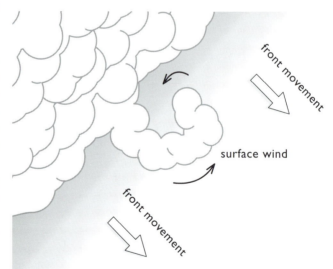

A line of thick clouds with an attached and distinctive hook or spiral represents an area of heavy precipitation and thunderstorms. Over land this can lead to tornadoes and over the ocean, to waterspouts. Downbursts can also be produced (for more on downbursts, see page 20). Actual tornadoes and waterspouts are normally too small to be easily identified using conventional radar.

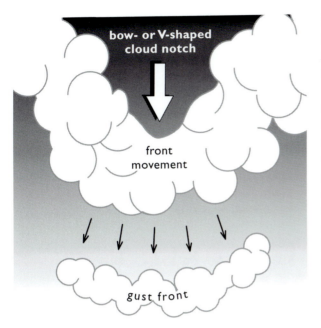

A bow or V-notch echo shows an area of concentrated winds and possible downburst activity. Radiating winds produce a gust front that can spawn squalls and tornadoes or waterspouts.

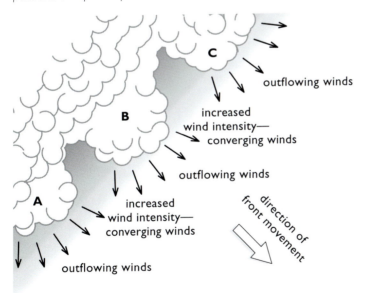

A typical squall line with areas A, B, and C representing concentrated storm cells. Storm cell areas will appear denser and larger than other portions of the squall line and will produce the strongest winds and rain.

indicate short-lived but often severe squalls and thunderstorms. The hooks and notches may be oriented in any direction. Dense and well-defined clouds indicate an intense system.

The clouds that accompany fronts and squalls are always cumulus with significant vertical development. Cumulonimbus (anvil-head) clouds are the most common type seen. Strong winds that come with the passage of an isolated squall are often preceded by a brief period of calm as winds flowing into the squall cloud are canceled out by winds moving out. Following this period of calm, strong and gusty winds fill in, with low cloud bases bringing the strongest wind.

The strongest winds that accompany a frontal system often precede the arrival of associated clouds. Just as a snowplow builds a wall of snow ahead of its blade, an approaching squall or front piles up and compresses air as it moves. This pileup often produces shifting and gusty winds several miles ahead of a cloud band.

An increase in air temperature, even a subtle change of a few degrees, accompanied by a recognizable cloud band on radar is often a signal of severe weather: temperature rises as air is compressed by an approaching front. Intense frontal passage is frequently accompanied by bands of parallel squall lines, which may not contain enough moisture to show up on radar. A leading squall line can often mask lines following behind.

A P P E N D I X
2

WEATHER CHECKLIST

Visual
Coastal Display

Combinations
Global Maritime Distress and Safety System (GMDSS)
Emergency Managers Weather Information Network (ENWIN)

Real-Time
Satellite Capture—POLAR/GOES
Internet: Buoy Data
Physical Oceanographic Real-Time System (PORTS)

Charts
Internet (http/ftp/e-mail)
WeatherFax (Wefax)

Voice
NOAA VHF Radio
USCG VHF Radio
HF, High Frequency (Single-Sideband) Voice
MF, Medium Frequency (Single-Sideband) Voice
Time Ticks
Amateur Radio (HAM)
Telephone

Text
Navtex
SITOR (Simplex Teletype over Radio)
Commercial E-mail
Inmarsat C

APPENDIX
3

RESOURCES

BOOKS

Bader, M. J., G. S. Forbes, J. R. Grant, R. B. E. Lilley, A. J. Waters. *Images in Weather Forecasting: A Practical Guide for Interpreting Satellite and Radar Imagery.* New York: Cambridge University Press, 1995.

Bluestein, Howard B. *Synoptic-Dynamic Meteorology in Midlatitudes.* New York: Oxford University Press, 1993.

Bowyer, Peter J. *Where the Wind Blows.* St. John's, NF: Breakwater Books Ltd., 1995.

Burgess, C. R., R. M. Frampton, and P. A. Uttridge. *Meteorology for Seafarers.* Glasgow: Brown, Son & Ferguson Ltd., 1988.

Burroughs, William J., Bob Crowder, Ted Robertson, Eleanor Vallier-Talbot, Richard Whitaker. *Weather.* New York: Nature Company/ Time Life Books, 1996.

Exploring the Environment through Satellite Imagery. McLean VA: Tri-Space Inc., 1994.

Mariners Weather Log. Silver Spring MD: National Weather Service (published three times annually).

Tufte, Edward R. *The Visual Display of Quantitative Information.* Cheshire CT: Graphics Press, 1983.

———. *Visual Explanations.* Cheshire CT: Graphics Press, 1997.

INTERNET ADDRESSES

The following Internet addresses can provide the information for your Weather Checklist. And these websites can lead you to more Internet links. There are also many other Internet sites of interest. Use one of the Internet search engines to search on topics such as marine weather, radiofax, radiofacsimile, weather buoys, and tides.

National Weather Service (NWS)

NWS Analysis and Forecast Products	http://www.nws.fsu.edu/wxhwy.html
NWS EMWIN (Emergency Managers Weather Information Network)	http://iwin.nws.noaa.gov/emwin/index.htm
NWS Environmental Modeling Center	http://nic.fb4.noaa.gov:8000
NWS Homepage	http://www.nws.noaa.gov
NWS ICNODDS (Internet Civilian Naval Oceanographic Data Distribution System)	http://cnodds.nws.noaa.gov
NWS Local Forecast Offices	http://www.nws.noaa.gov/regions.shtml
NWS Marine Charts	http://weather.noaa.gov/fax/marine.shtml
NWS Marine Prediction Center	http://www.ncep.noaa.gov/MPC
NWS Marine Product Dissemination	http://www.nws.noaa.gov/om/marine/home.htm
NWS Ocean Modeling Branch	http://polar.wwb.noaa.gov
NWS Marine Satellite Products	http://www.nws.noaa.gov/data.html#mar
NWS Publications	http://www.nws.noaa.gov/om/nwspub.htm
NWS WC/ATWC Tsunami Center	http://www.alaska.net/~atwc
NWS PTWC Tsunami Center	http://tgsv5.nws.noaa.gov/pr/hq/ptwc.htm
NWS Tropical Prediction Center	http://www.nhc.noaa.gov
NWS Tsunami Information Center	http://www.nws.noaa.gov/pr/hq/itic.htm
NWS VOS (Volunteer Observing Ship) Program	http://www.vos.noaa.gov

NWS Marine Prediction Center

MPCNWS Homepage	http://www.ncep.noaa.gov/
MPCNWS Tropical Prediction Center	http://www.nhc.noaa.gov
MPCNWS TPC Index Charts	http://www.nhc.noaa.gov/index.html

National Oceanic and Atmospheric Administration (NOAA)

NOAA Coastwatch	http://sgiot2.wwb.noaa.gov/COASTWATCH
NOAA Data Buoy Center	http://www.ndbc.noaa.gov/index.html
NOAA GOES	http://www.goes.noaa.gov
NOAA Homepage	http://www.noaa.gov
NOAA NCDC	http://www.ncdc.noaa.gov
NOAA NESDIS	http://ns.noaa.gov/NESDIS/NESDIS_Home.html
NOAA NODC	http://www.nodc.noaa.gov
NOAA Ports	http://www.opsd.nos.noaa.gov/d_ports.html
NOAA SEAS Program	http://dbcp.nos.noaa.gov/seas/seas.html
NOAA Tides & Currents	http://www.opsd.nos.noaa.gov
NOAA Weather Radio	http://www.nws.noaa.gov/nwr

U.S. Coast Guard

USCG CAMSLANT Comms	http://www.uscg.mil/lantarea/camslant
USCG CAMSPAC Comms	http://www.uscg.mil/pacarea/camspac/menu.html
USCG Homepage	http://www.uscg.mil
USCG International Ice Patrol	http://www.rdc.uscg.mil/iippages/home.html
USCG KODIAK Comms	http://www.ptialaska.net/~cskodiak/
USCG Maritime Telecommunications Information	http://www.navcen.uscg.mil/marcomms
USCG Navigation Center	http://www.navcen.uscg.mil

U.S. Navy

Naval Oceanographic Office	http://www.navo.navy.mil
Navy Fleet Numerical	http://www.fnmoc.navy.mil

NIMA (National Imagery and Mapping Agency)

Homepage	http://www.nima.mil

Information on GRIB Files

	http://www.comet.ucar.edu
	http://www.comet.ucar.edu/sac
	http://polar.wwb.noaa.gov/NEW.waves/Welcome.html

Information on Ice

National Ice Center	http://www.natice.noaa.gov
USCG International Ice Patrol	http://www.rdc.uscg.mil/iippages/home.html

Satellite E-Data

U.S. satellites:	
Ocean and Environmental Sensing (OCENS)	http://www.ocens.com
Other satellites:	http://celestrak.com
	http://www.rig.org.uk

WeatherFax

Listing of weatherfax stations:	http://ourworld.compuserve.com/homepages/HFFAX

Weather Model Outputs

Output from Rapid Update Cycle (RUC) model	http://www.marineweather.com

Decoded Offshore Weather Data

Penn State University	http://www.ems.psu.edu/cgi-bin/wx/offshore.cgi
World Meteorological Organization (WMO) Homepage	http://www.wmo.ch
International Maritime Organization (IMO) Homepage	http://www.imo.org

GLOSSARY

advection The horizontal transport of air or atmospheric properties. Commonly used with temperatures, as in warm-air advection.

advisory Advisories are issued for weather situations that cause significant inconveniences and could lead to life-threatening situations but do not meet warning criteria. Advisories are issued for events that are occurring, are imminent, or have a very high probability of occurrence.

air mass A homogeneous body of air with similar horizontal temperature and moisture characteristics which becomes modified if it moves over a different surface. Air masses are often separated by frontal surfaces.

anemometer An instrument that measures wind speed.

anticyclone *See* high-pressure system.

arc cloud Arc-shaped line of convective clouds associated with thunderstorms and fronts.

baroclinic leaf A distinctive cloud shape associated with development of midlatitude low-pressure systems.

barometer An instrument for measuring atmospheric pressure.

Beaufort scale A measurement of wind force, on a scale of 0 to 12, based upon sea state appearance.

blizzard Snow with winds in excess of 35 mph (30 knots) and visibilities of 1/4 mile or less for an extended period of time (e.g., more than three hours).

blowing dust Reduction of visibility by strong winds blowing across dry ground with little or no vegetation. A blowing dust advisory is issued when visibility is 1/8 mile or less over a widespread area.

broken clouds Clouds that cover between six-tenths and nine-tenths of the sky.

ceiling The height of the lowest layer of clouds when the sky is broken or overcast.

cirriform High-altitude ice clouds with a very thin, wispy appearance.

clear Sky condition of less than one-tenth cloud coverage.

climate The historical record of average daily and seasonal weather events.

closed low *See* cut-off low.

cloud streets Lines of disconnected clouds aligned with surface wind flow.

clutter Extraneous electronic data reflected off water molecules associated with ocean surface disturbances such as waves and atmospheric moisture.

coastal forecast A forecast of wind, wave, and weather conditions between the coastline and 25 miles offshore.

col Regions between high- and low-pressure systems where winds are light and clouds tend to form.

cold front The boundary between an advancing cold air mass and a relatively warmer air mass. Generally characterized by steady precipitation followed by showery precipitation. In the Northern Hemisphere, winds ahead of a cold front will be southwest and shift into the northwest with frontal passage. In the Southern Hemisphere, the corresponding wind shift is from the northeast to the northwest.

combined seas The combined height of swell and wind-generated waves.

comma cloud The signature comma shape on satellite images of the clouds typically associated with a low-pressure system.

complex low Area in which gale- or storm-force winds are forecast or are occurring and in which more than one center is generating winds.

condensation The process of gas changing to liquid.

continental air mass A dry air mass originating over a large land area.

convection Within a fluid such as air, the vertical movement of heat and moisture, especially by updrafts and downdrafts in an unstable atmosphere, creating a mixing motion. Towering cumulus clouds are visible forms of convection. The terms "convection" and "thunderstorms" are often used interchangeably, although thunderstorms are only one form of convection. When convection implies downward vertical motion, it is called *subsidence.*

Coriolis effect An apparent force caused by the rotation of the Earth. In the Northern Hemisphere winds are deflected to the right and in the Southern Hemisphere to the left, due to the Earth's rotation and spherical shape.

cut-off high A warm high that has become displaced and is on the polar side of a jet stream. It occurs mostly during spring and is frequent over northeastern Siberia, Alaska, and Greenland. A cut-off high is an example of a blocking high.

cut-off low A cold low that has become cut off from its associated jet stream and is on the equator side of the jet stream. It frequently occurs during spring and is often located over the southwestern United States and the northwestern coast of Africa.

cyclone *See* low-pressure system. (This is also the term used for a hurricane in the Indian Ocean and the western Pacific.)

dense fog advisory Issued when fog reduces visibility to $1/8$ mile or less over a widespread area.

depression A region of low pressure.

developing gale A low-pressure system where winds of 34 knots (39 mph) to 47 knots (54 mph) are expected.

developing storm A low-pressure system where winds of 48 knots (55 mph) or greater are expected.

dew point (or dew-point temperature) A measure of atmospheric moisture. Specifically, it is the temperature to which air must be cooled to reach saturation, for water vapor to condense and form dew, assuming constant air pressure and constant moisture content.

Doldrums *See* ITCZ.

downburst A severe localized downdraft from a convective parent cloud such as a thunderstorm.

drizzle Small, slowly falling water droplets, with diameters between 0.2 and 0.5 millimeters.

dry line The boundary separating moist and dry air masses, an important factor in severe-weather frequency. Severe thunderstorms often develop along a dry line, but the passing of a dry line typically produces clearing skies, a sharp drop in humidity, and a wind shift from the south or to the west.

duststorm Severe weather characterized by strong winds and dust-filled air over a large area. Visibility is reduced to between $5/8$ths and $5/16$ths of a statute mile.

e-data (ephemeris data) Mathematical data describing orbits of satellites, especially polar and geostationary satellites. Tracking systems need e-data to locate, capture, and process satellite images.

eddy A small disturbance of wind in a large wind flow, producing turbulent conditions. It is also an area of warmer air north of the westerlies or colder air south of the westerlies. (*See* cut-off high or cut-off low.) In oceanic circulation, an eddy is circular water movement formed where currents pass obstructions, between two counter-flowing adjacent currents or along the edge of a permanent current.

fair Less than four-tenths opaque cloud cover, no precipitation, and no extremes in temperature, visibility, or winds.

fetch The area in which ocean waves are generated by the wind. Also refers to the length of the fetch area, measured in the direction of the wind.

500-mb chart An upper-atmosphere chart showing the jet stream's location, strength, and direction of movement.

5,640 contour line A height contour line found on 500-mb upper-air charts showing the location and direction of movement for gale- and storm-force low-pressure systems. This line is also called the *storm track line.*

fog The visible aggregate of minute water droplets suspended in the atmosphere near the Earth's surface. Essentially, fog is a cloud whose base is at the Earth's surface.

forecast (prediction) A statement of expected future occurrences. Weather forecasting includes the use of objective models based on atmospheric parameters, along with the skill and experience of a meteorologist.

freezing level The altitude in the atmosphere where the temperature drops to 32°F.

freezing rain Rain which falls as liquid, then freezes upon impact, resulting in a coating of ice on exposed objects.

front The transition zone between two distinct air masses. The basic frontal types are cold, warm, stationary, and occluded fronts.

funnel cloud A rotating, cone-shaped column of air

extending downward from the base of a thunderstorm. When it reaches the ground, it is called a *tornado*.

gale A low-pressure system with sustained surface winds (duration of one minute) of 34 to 47 knots (39 to 54 mph).

geostationary satellite An orbiting weather satellite maintaining a constant position over the same area on the Earth's surface, about 23,000 miles directly over the equator, by matching the speed of the earth's rotation. It is often known as GOES, an acronym for Geostationary Operational Environmental Satellite.

geostrophic wind A steady horizontal motion of air along straight, parallel isobars or contours in an unchanging pressure field, resulting from combination of pressure gradient and Coriolis effect. It assumes no friction, a straight flow with no curvature, and no divergence or convergence.

GOES Geostationary Operational Environmental Satellite.

GRIB An acronym for Gridded Binary Data, a format used to process and transmit weather data.

ground fog Fog produced over the land by the cooling of the lower atmosphere as it comes in contact with the ground.

gust A brief sudden increase in wind speed. Generally the duration is less than 20 seconds and wind speed is roughly 50 percent greater than average wind speed.

gust front The leading edge of the downdraft from a thunderstorm.

hail Precipitation in the form of balls or irregular lumps of ice.

haze Fine dry or wet dust or salt particles in the air that reduce visibility.

high-pressure system An area of descending air moving outward and rotating clockwise in the Northern Hemisphere and counterclockwise in Southern Hemisphere. Also known as an *anticyclone*.

high wind Sustained winds greater than or equal to 40 mph (35 knots) or gusts greater than or equal to 58 mph (50 knots).

hook echo A radar return pattern associated with severe storms and tornadoes. Also referred to as a *spiral cloud*.

horse latitides The area near the equator—between 30 degrees North and 30 degrees South—this area has calm, light, and variable winds. Also known as the equatorial trough, the Intertropical Convergence Zone (ITCZ), or the Doldrums.

humidity The amount of water vapor in the atmosphere. (*See* relative humidity.)

hurricane A severe tropical low-pressure system with wind speeds in excess of 74 mph (64 knots) occurring in the Atlantic Ocean.

infrared (IR) Long-wave, electromagnetic radiation emitted by all hot objects. On the electromagnetic spectrum, IR is found between microwave radiation and visible light. Water vapor, ozone, and carbon dioxide are capable of absorbing or transmitting infrared radiation.

INMARSAT An acronym for the International Maritime Satellite System, a multinational organization providing weather, safety, and communications capabilities worldwide.

inversion An increase in temperature with height. The reverse of the normal cooling with height in the atmosphere.

IR Infrared satellite imagery. *See also* infrared (IR).

isobar A line connecting points of equal barometric pressure.

isopleth A line connecting points of equal value, also called an isoline. Isobars and isotherms are examples of isopleths.

isotherm A line connecting points of equal or constant air temperature.

ITCZ Intertropical Convergence Zone. Also known as the Doldrums, a belt of permanent low pressure near the equator where the northeasterly and southeasterly tradewinds converge, characterized by calm and variable winds accompanied by thunderstorms and squalls.

jet stream Strong upper-level winds concentrated within a narrow band in the atmosphere. The jet stream normally moves from west to east with a minimum speed of 50 knots and often exceeds 200 knots.

knot In marine applications, wind speed is measured in knots, nautical miles per hour (1 knot = 1.15 mph).

LAKI An acronym for the Limit of All Known Ice, which describes the boundaries of ice in a given area. The data are compiled from ship, aircraft, and radar reports.

land breeze. *See* offshore breeze.

likely In probability of precipitation statements, the equivalent of a 60 or 70 percent chance.

low-pressure system An area of converging and upward-moving air rotating counterclockwise in Northern Hemisphere and clockwise in Southern Hemisphere. Also known as a *cyclone*.

macroburst A large downburst with an outflow

diameter of 2.5 miles (4 km) or larger, containing damaging winds lasting up to 30 minutes.

macroscale   Meteorological scale covering an area ranging from the size of a continent to the entire globe.

maritime air mass   Moist air mass originating over the ocean.

mb   *See* millibar.

mesoscale   A size scale referring to weather systems that are smaller than synoptic-scale systems but larger than storm-scale systems. Horizontal dimensions range from 50 miles to several hundred miles. Squall lines are examples of mesoscale weather systems.

meteorology   The study of the atmosphere and atmospheric phenomena.

microburst   A strong localized downburst with an outflow diameter of 2.5 miles or less and peak gusts lasting 2 to 5 minutes.

microscale   The smallest scale of meteorological phenomena, ranging in size from a few centimeters to a few kilometers. Larger phenomena are classified as *mesoscale*. The term also refers to small-scale meteorological phenomena that have life spans of less than a few minutes, affect very small areas, and are strongly influenced by local conditions of temperature and terrain.

millibar   A unit of atmospheric pressure. 1 mb = 100 Pa (pascal). Normal surface pressure is approximately 1013 millibars.

monsoon   A seasonal shift of winds created by annual temperature variation occurring over large land areas in contrast with associated ocean surfaces. The word derived from *mausim*, Arabic for season. This weather pattern is most evident on southern and eastern sides of Asia—it is often associated with moisture and copious rains that arrive with southwest flow across southern India—but it does occur elsewhere, such as in the southwestern United States.

MPC   Marine Prediction Center.

National Centers For Environmental Prediction (NCEP)   As part of the National Weather Service, these centers provide timely, accurate, and continually improving worldwide forecasts. Centers include the Aviation Weather Center, Climate Prediction Center, Storm Prediction Center, and Tropical Prediction Center. For more information, contact the NCEP central offices in Silver Spring, Maryland.

National Weather Service (NWS)   The primary branch of the National Oceanic and Atmospheric Administration, responsible for all aspects of observing and forecasting atmospheric conditions and their consequences, including severe weather and flood warnings.

nautical mile (nm)   Used in marine navigation, the unit of length equal to a minute of arc of a great circle. One nautical mile equals 1.151 statute miles (1.852 km) or 6,076 feet.

NOAA   National Oceanic and Atmospheric Administration. A branch of the U.S. Department of Commerce, NOAA is the parent organization of the National Weather Service.

NOAA Weather Radio   Continuous, 24-hour-a-day VHF broadcasts of weather observations and forecasts directly from National Weather Service offices. A special tone allows certain receivers to sound an alarm when watches or warnings are issued.

north wall   The northern edge or boundary of a major ocean current, located where significant temperature gradients and the strongest currents are found or where the highest waves occur while the wind blows against a current flow. The north wall is often associated with Gulf Stream and Kuroshio currents.

numerical forecasting or **numerical weather prediction (NWP)**   Forecasting weather by the use of numerical models, such as equations of hydrodynamics subjected to observed initial conditions. Models, such as RUC, Aviation, and MRF, are run on high-speed computers at the National Centers for Environmental Prediction.

NWS   National Weather Service.

occluded front   A complex frontal system that occurs when a cold front overtakes a warm front. Also known as an *occlusion*.

offshore breeze   A local wind that blows from the land toward a body of water, caused by unequal heating and cooling of land and water. Also known as a *land breeze*.

offshore forecast   A marine weather forecast for the waters between 25 and 250 nautical miles off the coast.

omega block   Upper-level ridges that have pronounced north–south development and resemble the Greek letter omega (Ω).

onshore breeze   A local wind that blows from a body of water toward the land, caused by unequal heating and cooling of land and water. Also known as a *sea breeze*.

overcast   Sky condition when greater than nine-tenths of the sky is covered.

partly cloudy   Sky condition when between three- and seven-tenths of the sky is covered.

polar front Boundary between polar air and air from low latitudes where a majority of depressions develop.

polar low A small and often intense low-pressure system forming when very cold and dry polar continental air moves over warmer ocean waters. Wind speeds often reach storm and hurricane strength.

polar orbiting satellite A satellite that circles the Earth from pole to pole at an altitude of about 500 miles, making a complete circumnavigation every 100 minutes, during which time the Earth has rotated 25 degrees.

precipitation Liquid or solid water molecules that fall from the atmosphere and reach the ground.

pressure The force exerted by the interaction of the atmosphere and gravity. Also known as *atmospheric pressure*.

pressure gradient The difference in pressure between two points as related to their distance apart. Surface weather charts use isobar lines to show pressure gradient.

radiation fog *See* ground fog.

radiosonde An instrument attached to a weather balloon that transmits data on pressure, humidity, temperature, and winds as it ascends.

rain Liquid water droplets that fall from the atmosphere, having diameters greater than drizzle (greater than 0.5 mm).

rapidly intensifying low (RIL) Severe low-pressure systems with a surface pressure drop of 24 mb or more within 24 hours.

relative humidity The amount of water vapor in the air compared to the amount the air could hold if it were saturated (expressed as a percentage).

ridge An elongated area of high pressure at the surface or aloft.

roll cloud A relatively rare, low-level, horizontal, tube-shaped cloud. Although associated with a thunderstorm, it is completely detached from the base of a cumulonimbus cloud.

rope cloud A long and narrow band of clouds seen on satellite imagery and associated with cold fronts.

Rossby waves The movement of ridges and troughs in upper wind patterns—primarily the jet stream—circling the earth. Named for Carl-Gustaf Rossby, a U.S. Weather Bureau (NWS) employee, who first theorized about the existence of the jet stream in 1939.

RUC Rapid Update Cycle model, generated every three hours.

satellite pictures Taken by a weather satellite, pictures revealing information, such as the flow of water vapor, movement of frontal systems, and the development of tropical systems. Looping individual pictures together helps meteorologists forecast the weather. The satellites capture images in VIS (visible) and IR (infrared) spectrums.

scattered clouds Sky condition when between one- and five-tenths is covered.

sea breeze *See* onshore breeze.

sea state The conditions on open water resulting from wind flow combined with sea and swell direction, height, and period.

sea surface temperature Surface temperature data collected from buoy, ship, and IR satellite images.

severe thunderstorm A strong thunderstorm with wind gusts in excess of 58 mph (50 knots) and/or hail with a diameter of $3/4$ inch or more.

shear Variation in wind speed or direction over a short distance and over a short time. Shear usually refers to vertical wind shear, but the term also describes changes in horizontal velocity over short distances.

shower Precipitation that is intermittent in time, area, or intensity.

significant wave height Average height of highest third of all waves in a given area.

sleet A type of frozen precipitation consisting of small, transparent pellets.

slight chance In probability of precipitation statements, generally equivalent to a 20 percent chance.

small craft advisory Advisory issued when winds between 22 knots (25 mph) and 34 knots (39 mph) may cause hazardous conditions for operators of small vessels, which are generally defined as vessels under 65 feet in length.

snow Frozen precipitation composed of ice particles in complex hexagonal patterns.

snow advisory An advisory issued when snow is expected to create hazardous conditions and hamper travel; a winter storm advisory warns of more severe conditions.

snow flurries Light snow showers, usually of an intermittent nature with no measurable accumulation.

squall line A non-frontal line of concentrated and strong convective activity characterized by thunderstorms and strong, shifting winds.

stationary front A transition zone between air masses when neither is advancing upon the other.

storm In marine usage, a low-pressure system with winds 48 knots (55 mph) or greater.

storm surge A rise of the sea preceding a storm (usually a hurricane) due to the winds generated and low atmospheric pressure.

storm track   The path followed across the earth's surface by storm systems, such as midlatitude low-pressure systems. A storm track is depicted on upper air (500-mb) charts using a darkened 5,640 height contour.

straight-line winds   Thunderstorm winds most often associated with the gust front. They originate from downdrafts and can cause damage in a "straight line," as opposed to tornadic wind damage, which has circular characteristics.

streamline charts   Tropical analysis and forecast charts that use lines showing prevailing wind flow in place of isobar lines.

subsidence   Sinking air that is warmed upon approaching the Earth's surface, producing little cloud formation.

subtropical jet   The branch of the jet stream that is found in the lower latitudes.

surge area   Bands of clouds and precipitation ahead of an active surface cold front.

sustained winds   The wind speed obtained by averaging the observed values over a one-minute period.

swells   Regular ocean waves of longer duration than wind waves.

synoptic scale (or large scale)   The size scale of high- and low-pressure systems, in the lower troposphere, that cover several hundred miles or more. Most high- and low-pressure areas are synoptic-scale systems. Compare with *mesoscale.*

thermal   Small, rising column of air due to surface heating.

thunderstorm   A storm with lightning and thunder, produced by a cumulonimbus cloud, usually producing gusty winds, heavy rain, and sometimes hail.

tornado   A violent rotating column of air, in contact with the ground, pendant from a cumulonimbus cloud. A tornado can exist without a visible funnel cloud.

tradewinds   Persistent tropical winds that blow from the subtropical high-pressure centers towards the equatorial low.

tropical depression   A tropical low-pressure system with cyclonic wind circulation, and winds between 20 and 34 knots.

tropical disturbance   An organized mass of tropical thunderstorms, with a slight cyclonic circulation and winds less than 20 knots.

tropical storm   A developed tropical low-pressure system with winds between 34 and 63 knots.

trough   An elongated area of low pressure at the surface or aloft. Written as "trof" on weather charts.

turbulence   Disrupted flow in the atmosphere that produces gusts and eddies.

typhoon   A hurricane that originates in the western Pacific Ocean.

upper air/upper level   The portion of the atmosphere above the lower troposphere, above 850 millibars. Therefore, upper-level lows and highs, troughs, winds, observations, and charts all apply to atmospheric phenomena above surface.

upper-level system   Large-scale or mesoscale disturbances capable of producing upward motion (lift) in the middle or upper parts of the atmosphere.

VIS   Visible-spectrum satellite imagery.

visibility   The horizontal distance an observer can see and identify a prominent object.

V-notch   The shape located on the backside of strong lows and apparent on satellite images where cold air is descending and funneling into the system, inhibiting cloud development.

vorticity   A measure of spin, or rotation, within areas of low and high pressure, used to gauge the intensity of developing systems.

warm front   A boundary between a warm air mass and a cooler air mass it is displacing.

warning   Forecast issued when a particular hazard is imminent or already occurring (e.g., a tornado warning).

watch   Forecast issued well in advance to alert the public of the possibility of a particular hazard (e.g., a flash flood watch).

waterspout   A small and short-lived spinning system occurring over water and associated with warm sea and air temperatures and low cloud bases. In essence, a tornado over water.

wind advisory   An advisory of sustained winds 25 to 39 mph (22 to 34 knots) and/or gusts to 57 mph (50 knots), normally limited to a certain area. Wind advisories may not be issued for areas that routinely experience winds of this magnitude (e.g., the strong summer winds near the San Francisco Bay would not trigger an advisory).

wind waves   Irregular waves of short period created by the flow of air over the water.

winter storm   A heavy-snow event. Below 7,000 feet, a snow accumulation of more than 6 inches per 12 hours or more than 12 inches per 24 hours; above 7,000 feet, more than 8 inches per 12 hours or more than 18 inches per 24 hours.

INDEX